JOURNAL FOR THE STUDY OF THE OLD TESTAMENT
SUPPLEMENT SERIES
35

Editors
David J A Clines
Philip R Davies

Department of Biblical Studies
The University of Sheffield
Sheffield S10 2TN
England

SAGA
LEGEND
TALE
NOVELLA
FABLE

Narrative Forms in
Old Testament
Literature

Edited by
George W. Coats

Journal for the Study of the Old Testament
Supplement Series 35

Published by
JSOT Press
Department of Biblical Studies
The University of Sheffield
Sheffield S10 2TN
England

Printed in Great Britain
by Redwood Burn Ltd.,
Trowbridge, Wiltshire.

British Library Cataloguing in Publication Data

Saga, legend, fable, tale, novella : narrative
    forms in Old Testament literature.—(Journal
    for the study of the Old Testament supplement series,
    ISSN 0309-0787; 35)
    1. Bible. O.T.—Criticism, interpretation, etc.
    I. Coats, George W.   II. Series
    221.6   BS1171.2

ISBN 0-905774-84-1
ISBN 0-905774-85-X Pbk

CONTENTS

Introduction

GENRES: WHY SHOULD THEY BE IMPORTANT FOR EXEGESIS?

George W. Coats

Many objects of our interest fall into classification groups. Plants belong to a genus and species. Animals can be grouped according to characteristics that identify families. It is relevant to know whether an object of interest, say a set of bones discovered from the ancient world, belonged to an animal of the bovine or equine class. To know something of the class would obviously help in establishing what the animal was and why it might have been where it was. Even inanimate objects can be grouped according to class. A building may be obviously a private dwelling, an office building, or a public assembly hall. If architecture is the general area of study, it would be obviously necessary for students to know whether the object under consideration would fall into one of the groups of structures the field of study normally deals with and how the particular object might relate to the general group. If students want to draw plans for their buildings, they would not do so in a haphazard way. They would draw something that would fit with the class of their assignment. Otherwise, the bridge might fall, the assembly hall might be too small, or the private dwelling might be unfit for supporting the life of a family. Archaeologists classify the pieces of pottery they discover in their exploration according to shape, function, or decoration. And the classification helps them determine the contribution of the shard to the total picture of the tell's history.

The same point can be made about literature. It makes some difference in how we read a piece of writing if we know in advance whether the writing is a business letter from the bishop of the church, an advertisement from the local pest control firm, or a love letter from that very special sweetheart. In literature of the classical sort, a piece might be a drama, a comedy in three acts. And every student of

Shakespeare will understand that the comedy will not necessarily provoke laughter in all three acts. Its generic quality is different, a series of events centered around a principal figure and his supporters that leads finally to a peaceful resolution for the principal. In OT narratives, not all pieces belong to the same class. Some can be grouped according to similar construction techniques. Some can be grouped according to the place in Israel's society that gave them purpose and life. Some can be grouped together because they fulfill roughly the same or at least related goals for the public who witnessed them. And the grouping, when organized according to clear principles, can be quite precise. A saga is not the same thing as a legend, nor a fable the same as history.

The point of genre study must, however, be quite clear from the beginning. The point is not to facilitate a 'name game'. It is possible to conclude, after some survey of the literature on genre studies, that the primary goal for the study is to develop the right name for the object of the probe. If scholars can agree on a label, a convenient term useful for reference to the object of study, then the goal of the genre exercise will be complete. Thus, it would make no real difference whether the term 'saga' has credibility in contemporary scholarship. The point would be to discover a definition that all could subscribe to and then use the term with consistency. Or, from the other side of the question, it would make no real difference whether the term 'saga' has credibility in contemporary scholarship. The point would be to uncover the plethora of conflicting usages for the term and then to discredit all definitions and thus the term itself. Both alternatives belong to a game played by scholars in the name of literary research. But the goal of genre studies is not simply to defend the right use of a name. It is rather to identify a class of literature that will facilitate a functional definition of any given piece that may belong to the class. It will show how the literature that appears in the class functioned in the context of its original place in the world of people. It will show what needs or goals that literature fulfilled and how that task was met. The point of genre study is thus connected intrinsically with the goals of interpretation. In the same way that a biologist might ask of a set of bones what kind of animal lay at the living point, so the literary artist might ask of a set of literary bones what kind of literature lay at the living point in the history of the art. To answer the question about class would put the art critic in the proper place to seek out further issues of interpretation.

A few illustrations might help make the point. If I as a minister of the United Methodist Church receive a letter from the local bishop of the church regarding my next appointment, it might make some difference in the way I handle the letter if I should assume that the letter contains an advertisement for the local pest control services. To make a false judgment about genre might lead me to throw away an important piece of mail that could prove absolutely essential for my professional future. In any kind of effort to interpret something, whatever it may be, some kind of assumption will be made about class. The point is not whether in the process of interpretation some classification should occur. It will occur. The point is to raise the classification process to a conscious level so that it might be carefully controlled. If the classification process has been done self-consciously, then I would not throw away a critical letter from the bishop.

The conclusion that I must draw from these general reflections about classification is that classification of an object into its typical group facilitates the process of interpretation. I can perceive the proper use of a particular car if I can see the proper use of its class. If I buy a car out of the general class where the goals I have in mind properly fit, then I cannot be too surprised when my particular new car fails to meet the goals I have in mind. If I choose the form of a love letter to guide the construction of my letter to the bishop, I should not be too surprised when not only my petition to the bishop fails but also my position in the church falls into jeopardy as a result of my intemperate approach to the church's leader. The proper genre must be chosen if a particular goal is to be met. Or to put the point in a different way, since in order to meet a particular goal, one must choose the appropriate instrument, the right tool, the right car, the right building, the right piece of writing, the task of interpretation can be enhanced by reversing the process. By asking what goals a particular genre can meet, the interpreter can discover what immediate goals the artist responsible for a particular piece of interest might have had for his creation. The genre is designed to meet a particular function. And a careful writer—or a careful interpreter of a written piece—will be aware of the genre intrinsic for the piece he is interested in.

There is consistently a correspondence between the genre that serves to present some particular content to the world and the intention for the content. Indeed, there is a clear correspondence between the typical genre and the unique content of any given piece of literature. To be aware of the genre, thus the kind or class of expression used to present the unique content, will give a precise handle for controlling what the point of the content may be. This point may be illustrated one step further by casting the following scenario: On July 4, 1981, the political fortunes of a local candidate were celebrated on the steps of the county courthouse. In order to set the tone for the celebration the local high school band was invited to play. The candidate did not want a standard pep rally, however. He wanted classical music, appropriate for the classical style of leadership he intended to establish. Thus, in order to meet the tastes of the candidate, the band played its own rendition of Beethoven's requiem mass. The event appropriately marked the beginning of the candidate's decline, for the genre of the music, requiem mass, is intended to meet the needs of a funeral. Interpretation of the music, the act that would have been necessary in order to determine whether the music was appropriate for the occasion, failed to perceive that the genre was not intended to function at a political rally. Thus, to ask about the genre of a piece is not simply a game of names. It is a process of interpretation that enables a critic to know what the function of the piece is, what goals it can fulfill, what intentions it can facilitate. That goal applies whether the critics are searching for the right genre to meet their own needs or interpreting a piece used by someone else, moving toward the goal of understanding the user's purposes and intentions.

The illustration marks an additional facet of genre studies, however. To make false assumptions about genre can lead to gross misunderstanding. If a politician chooses a funeral piece to mark the beginning of his campaign, he will have erred in his communication of political style to his constituency. If the interpreter assumes the genre to be of one class but in fact it is of another class, that person will be subject to the same error. If, on the other hand, the interpreter can raise the assumptions about genre to a conscious level and control them with discipline, then that person will be in a much better position to make an accurate judgment about the object of interest.

There is an additional problem that must be considered as a critical element in any evaluation of genre studies. Some pieces of literature—or any other kind of object—may be genuinely unique, not readily subject to classification in a group. This kind of object may result from a conscious alteration of the characteristics at home in the genre. Thus, the high school band leader may have chosen consciously to play a requiem mass for a political leader whose position he opposes. He breaks the genre by changing the setting the genre originally appeared in and thus he gives the piece a unique intention. The author's freedom to employ the genre in new and creative ways must not be overlooked. Moreover, the artist may create a piece whose characteristics fail to correspond to any class. The requiem mass at a political rally would still show signs of the genre. Indeed, it would be precisely the characteristic signs of the genre that would give the piece its unique punch in the political pep rally. But the artist may also create a piece that breaks all characteristics of the genre. The piece may appear as something quite new, quite different. Genre study depends on finding the typical in a piece of literature. But it can also facilitate identification of the unique, simply by enabling the critic to discover what elements of a piece do not correspond to the class. And the unique would serve the task of interpretation by setting the context for the intention of an individual piece of art.

Thus, the task of the interpreter is not to foreclose on the creativity of an artist at any given point, the ability of an artist to use a genre in a new setting or to add elements of content that might conflict with the genre. The task of the interpreter who uses genre study as an entry into the field of meaning resident in the object of interest knows that the task is descriptive, not normative. When a piece of art appears that does not match the ideal form of the genre, the interpreter has no right to reconstruct the piece according to a predetermined, ideal genre. The task is rather to describe the unique piece for what it is. Then, if it matches the genre, some conclusion about its role in the class can be drawn. If it does not, then new categories must be sought, or perhaps in some cases, the distinctive role for the unique must be identified.

If genre studies are so crucial for the process of interpretation, it would be all the more important to understand what a genre is. What precisely constitutes a genre? One can conclude that a genre of literature in the OT has been identified adequately when the following elements emerge as in some sense typical:

1. *A typical structure.* A genre, a general class of various pieces of literature, might properly be identified when the various members of the class reflect a common pattern of structure. Any object of art such as we have been considering, just like any object with some utilitarian purpose, will have a structure. A bridge may be suspension

in structure. Or it may have pillars at key points along the course of its span. The structure reflects the pattern of its construction. An engine may have several cylinders to propel the drive shaft. The position of the cylinders in a series or in complementary opposite arrangement would reflect its structure, the pattern of its construction. A piece of literature will have various parts, related to each other in a functional pattern. The relationship facilitates the public presentation of the content in the piece and shows something about the tendency of those parts to communicate the content. These relationships can be defined as the structure of the piece. And if the relationships can be identified in more than one piece of literature, the structure will be in some sense typical, a key facet in identification of the genre. An example of characteristic structure as a key for identifying the genre is the narrative form called legend. The legend will emphasize a virtue as a critical element in the structure of the whole unit (see the discussion of legend by Ron Hals in Chapter 1).

2. *A typical vocabulary.* A genre might again reveal a tendency to employ a standard group of words or phrases. If the assumption is that a genre is the best form for presenting a particular body of content, and that genre and content correspond, then it would be a natural consequence that standard vocabulary would function to accomplish the typical goals of the genre. Thus, for example, in the prophetic oracle of judgment, the two parts of structure, the indictment and the sentence, typically break at a point marked with a stereotyped 'therefore' (*lākēn*). The word itself becomes a standard marker for the genre. Indeed, the word becomes a key for marking the major elements of structure in the genre. Thus, this facet of the definition of genre stands in some respects in the service of the preceding facet. Typical vocabulary will help identify the patterns of a typical structure.

In narrative genres, vocabulary also plays a critical role for identifying the structure of a unit. Vocabulary in these cases may not be so strictly stereotyped as in the cases of particular prophetic speeches. Yet, typical expressions, formulaic constructs, will serve to mark the patterns of structure. For example, the narrative formulas marking that element of structure called exposition carry standard vocabulary, such as *wayᵉhî* (so Gen 26.1). And similar patterns can occur within a story but as a marker for structure, such as *wayᵉhî kaʾᵃšer . . .* (so Gen 27.30).

Typical vocabulary may also emerge in relationship to the typical content characteristically carried by the genre. The typical vocabulary may therefore be simply a consequence of the rule of thumb that a genre will serve standard content. Thus, again, the standard vocabulary may be nothing more than an extension of other characteristics in the definition of genre, the characteristic structure, or the characteristic content.

3. *A typical setting.* Setting refers to the place in society where a piece of literature most naturally belongs, lives. The category applies not only to a particular piece of literature, but to the broader classification of types or genres for its group.

A genre, properly identified, will reflect use in the creative womb of a particular setting. Indeed, the function of the genre will normally emerge most clearly by reference to the goals accomplished by the genre within the setting. Thus, the music for requiem mass fulfills its purposes most adequately if it is executed in the context of the great cathedral at the moment of celebration for the life of a person whose death now must be observed. It is clear, also, that while a genre may belong to a particular setting and most naturally fill its role there, the author of any given piece may use the genre out of its setting. That movement would in itself give the interpreter a creative hold on interpretation, for it would suggest something about the particular intention of the piece. If, for example, the requiem mass were performed at the political rally to celebrate the inauguration of a candidate's campaign, the shift in natural setting for the genre tells what the intention in the particular performance may be.

4. *A typical function.* A genre will serve to fulfill a typical function. This point reflects the general rule of thumb that genre and content correspond in order to accomplish a particular, recurring goal. Indeed, some clear distinction can be noted at this point between the terms intention and function. The genre fulfills a function within its setting. When the genre is given life by combination with particular content, the typical function of the genre will meet a particular intention. The individual piece of literature will have accomplished its goals, its intention, in accord with the typical function of the genre it represents.

Thus, the general question may be addressed directly. Why should the student of exegesis ask about genres? If a genre observation isolates characteristics that are fundamentally a part of the unit under consideration, and if those characteristics can be identified in other pieces of literature, then the common patterns of the pieces can come to light. Moreover, the common patterns will show a tendency for the genre, a tendency that illuminates the typical function of the genre. The student of exegesis can then ask whether the particular piece under investigation also reveals the generic function or some distinct, unique function. These fruits open the particular intention of the piece, and they arise primarily from investigation of genre. The following collection of essays focuses on narrative genres. The assumption is that generic qualities can be readily uncovered in narrative tradition, perhaps more readily than in the more particularistic pieces of literature from poetic sources such as Job or Ecclesiastes. The choice is in the final analysis, however, arbitrary. The value of the question might be as readily set forward from the poetry of the psalms as the prose of the narrative books.

Moreover, the narrative genres considered here share a distinguishing characteristic. One group of narrative genres would, in some manner, report events or data from the past simply to record the past. The genres in that group could not offer the interpreter a guarantee of historical accuracy in particular details or even in the general sequence of events. But they would present their material in order to affirm that for the narrator the events in fact occurred in a particular way. These genres would, as a rule of thumb, be descriptive. They describe the events that comprise the content of the communication, or they report the data that lie at the center of their concerns. The structure of the genre would thus be dictated by the cause-effect sequence of the events or simply by the particular details in the subject of the description.

The other group of narrative genres, the group represented by this collection, intends to tell a story so that the telling will capture the attention of the audience and facilitate communication of the storyteller's particular point. The story may develop its pattern from events that actually happened in the past, or from events the storyteller believes to have happened in the past. But the genre would not be designed simply to describe the events. The structure of the genre would not be dictated by the cause-effect sequence of the events or a simple report of details in the events. The structure would be dictated by the goals of the storyteller for developing a plot to hold the attention of the audience or a program to establish a special cause important for the storyteller. The storyteller would be free to shape the material of the narrative according to a design that would most adequately accomplish the particular goals latent in the storytelling event. Thus, the accuracy and historicity of the story would not be the key element for evaluation of the unit. The key element would be the success or failure in the narrative's move toward its climax. The question for the critic is not what might have happened that captured the attention of the storyteller. The question concerns the style of the storyteller's art. Why did the storyteller tell the story in just this particular way and not in some other way?

Our contemporary standards of judgment should not color valuations for that kind of storytelling. We are prepared normally to conclude that any story that shapes the facts from the past in order to make the storyteller's goals more readily attainable deserves the label of falsehood, a deception, a distortion of the truth. But judgments about a particular story's ability to depict truth should not rest on the ability of the genre to represent facts from the past as they might have actually happened. If the function of the genre is to do that, then the tendency of our modern judgments would be appropriate. But if the function of the genre is to paint a story for other purposes, then the story must be judged for its success or failure in meeting its own purposes.

The plan of the following collection calls thus for essays that present a theoretical definition of the genre, and then for complementary essays that demonstrate the value of the genre definition for exegesis of a particular text. The goal of the collection is to show that interpretation advances under the careful control of genre definition.

1

SAGA

Robert W. Neff

Imprecision in the classification of literary genres has caused an increasing restiveness among form critical investigators of the Old Testament. Scholars have commonly expressed 'dissatisfaction with terms such as saga, legend, historical narrative, and the like',[1] and spoken to the hidden doubts about terminology that many of us held. Ron Hals has analysed the great confusion in the use of legend and saga and has called for a reassessment of the ways in which we use these terms.[2] As early as 1964, Claus Westermann suggested that we should give up using the term 'Saga'[3] and John van Seters has asserted that saga is a misnomer for the Genesis material.[4] Gene Tucker has exhibited a similar restiveness about saga but has nevertheless concluded, 'It seems best to continue to use the term saga while at the same time attempting to determine what is distinctive and characteristic about the sagas of the Old Testament'.[5] Clearly we need to reexamine the term saga and its usefulness for genre identification.

In the current state of the debate I would expect that the members of the scholarly community anticipate that I have written to bury saga and not to praise it. It is not the purpose of this paper to present a funeral oration since I am not yet convinced that we are dealing with a corpse. Rather I would suggest that we examine the reasons for terminological problems, particularly in the work of Gunkel, Jolles, and Westermann, and then describe the Icelandic sagas to determine whether the characteristics of that literature are shared by the narratives of Genesis. The first question is simply, 'Does the term saga (Saga)[6] refer to a distinct literary genre and if so, what are the characteristics of that genre?' And the second question is, 'Do narratives in Genesis share those characteristics in great enough degree to be called sagas?'

.

I

In his commentary on Genesis, Gunkel defines *Sage* as 'folkloristic, traditional, poetic narrative which treats persons or events of the past'[7] and gives five distinctive marks of *Sage*:

1. The principal mark is that the saga circulated originally as oral tradition.[8]
2. The saga speaks of things which are close to the hearts of the folk, of the personal and private.[9]
3. It was different with saga, which derives its material only in part out of tradition, but in part out of fantasy. No particular person was present at the creation, no human tradition reaches to the time of the origin of our kind (humankind), to primeval people or primeval language.[10]
4. The clearest mark of the saga is that it commonly reports of things that for us are unbelievable.[11]
5. The saga however is according to its nature poetry: it pleases, exalts, inspires, moves.[12]

These marks have often been recited by most of us when we attempt to define *Sage*; they appear in Tucker's definition of saga and are virtually the same as those tabulated by Klatt.[13]

These marks actually grew out of Gunkel's first question, 'Does Genesis relate history or *Sage*?'[14] The overriding issue in defining *Sage* became the demarcation of *Sage* from 'Geschichte' (story/history). In part Gunkel inherited this problem from the literary science of his day, since the Grimm brothers in their *Wörterbuch* remarked of *Sage*, 'In the older languages the idea of the unhistorical remains connected indissolubly with the concept of *Sage*'.[15] In part he was setting forth his ideas in the context of a theological debate where he wanted to maintain the meaning and significance of these narratives when they were judged to be 'poetry' rather than 'prose and history'.[16] Although Gunkel did not want to suggest that *Sage* was unhistorical, nonetheless in his work this genre emerges by way of comparison with history.

The criteria for the genre *Sage* in Gunkel's work emerge when two genres are defined vis-à-vis one another. For example, if history is written, then *Sage* is not written. If history deals with the great public events, then *Sage* deals with the inner lives of families and tribes. If history is prose, then *Sage* is poetry. One ends up with a tautology: History is not *Sage*; and *Sage* is not History. Richter points to this problem:

> Gunkel now begins, if still a little cautiously, with an evaluation of the genre from the standpoint of the historian, without considering other standpoints, by dividing the narrative genres into two groups.[17]

Unfortunately the horizon of the historian overshadows Gunkel's definition of *Sage*.

A further weakness arises when one examines certain key words in the definition. *Sage* is oral tradition. The basic definition of *Sage* remains 'das, was gesagt ist', 'That which was said'. John van Seters attacks this use of the term because it places an inordinate weight on the oral stage of narratives which now appear in written form. The validity of this attack emerges more clearly when we consider the observations of Northrop Frye that 'the basis of generic distinctions in literature appears to be the radical of presentation'.[18] Although one should be careful not to take this distinction too far, by the use of *Sage* we are always pressed beyond the written form to one which lies behind it. The written stage of the material is not accounted for in the definition.

When one considers another fundamental mark of the genre such as *Poesie*, one discovers the illusiveness of the definition. Gunkel does not have in mind metrical writing. He cannot since the *Sagen* he had in mind are in prose. Rather *Poesie* refers to the poetic, the non-prosaic, the deep feelings about personal matters. We are touching the romantic impulse of the master which led him to make many accurate observations but hardly a vocabulary which will be helpful in defining a particular genre. *Poesie* becomes a weasel word which easily can lead astray.

The problem becomes more acute when one examines the criteria for the recognition of a particular genre, which according to Gunkel are:

1. a certain field of thoughts and definitions.
2. a clear language of the form in which these are expressed.
3. a setting in life, out of which only content and form can be understood.[19]

Of the five marks listed by Gunkel for recognizing *Sage*, four generally apply to the first category. The fifth mark (see above) does not imply a clear *Formensprache* since as Klatt correctly observes, 'For "poetic Tone" does not mean linguistic elements of form, rules of elements or structure, but much more the vitality of the saga'.[20] This means that for Gunkel's second criterion there are no corresponding identifiable marks within the Gattung *Sage*.

A second problem appears when we wrestle with the question of *Sitz im Leben*. Since Gunkel localizes this genre in the oral tradition of the folk, we have at best a general setting for *Sage* which defies a more explicit definition. The definition presupposes an oral folk narrative and yet we have no handles for getting at it. How could one localize story-telling anyway? We are left with the most general rubric which defies a more specific institutional or sociological setting.

When we use the marks that Gunkel has outlined for the recognition of *Sage*, we are basically dealing with logical and not narrative categories. This means that *Sage* becomes a genre for expressing certain kinds of thought and is indicative of a pre-national or pre-historical mentality without at the same time judging the veracity of its content. We will note this pre-national orientation for the definition of *Sage* or its equivalent in the work of Jolles and Westermann. Gunkel's definition of *Sage* can no longer be considered adequate for genre identification.

II

Jolles delineates three types of saga which have emerged in Iceland:

1. *Islendinga saga*. Narratives concerning the Icelandic settlers, their neighbors and contemporaries, their origin, their relationship to each other . . . In them is told how a particular family built its house and court, how it took possession of the family property . . . how many sons and daughters it numbered, from where the sons took their wives, where the daughters found their husbands.[21]

2. *Kings' saga*. These royal narratives are very different from what we would call political history. The king acts as a north-German king: he is a Viking, he conquers, he does battle; but everything that we would attribute to the concept of the state is missing. He goes to battle as an individual, as a member of the family . . .[22]

3. *Fornaldar saga*. In the first place it is much less closely linked

together in time or place. It includes material from a period
well before the settlement of Iceland. It know of heroes who
were not originally connected with Iceland or indeed with the
north-Germans. And finally, these narratives extend further
and narrate matters which we would generally assign to other
Gattungen, which cannot indeed be located in place or time,
Gattungen which had their inception very much earlier and
very much further away from us.[23]

Jolles contends that the first form created the Vorbild for the other
two.

This latter observation becomes important, since Jolles's definition
of Saga will derive from this first form. He asks what is essential to
the Islendinga Saga and answers: 'The inner structure of the
Icclandic Saga is conditioned by the idea of family'.[24] It is the bond
of blood which binds people together in the saga.[25] Therefore, we
find the relationships of father to son, grandfather to grandson,
brother to brother, brother to sister, and husband to wife.[26] However,
the men in the Islendinga sogur do not build a nation or a state but
contribute to the development of a family line which gains in honor
and power. He concludes his definition with the assertion: 'In the
case of Saga, we allude to a preoccupation with the terms family,
clan, blood, relationship'.[27]

Having defined *Sage* in this way, Jolles sought to discover whether
any other culture produced this form. References to particular
families do appear in the Iliad and the Nibelunglied. In Book II of the
Iliad (lines 100ff.), the family of Pelops appears as a distinct entity
apart from the Greek nation just as the families of Nibelungen,
Walisungen, and Gibuchungen stood apart from any national identity
now presupposed in the Nibelungenlied. These brief accounts indicate
for Jolles that a *Sage* of the family of Pelops and a *Sage* of Nibelungen
or the Walisungen did exist. However, the transition from *Sage* (oral
narrative) to saga (written narrative) did not take place in Greece and
in Germany.[28] The Epic overshadowed the *Sage* and thus its written
evidence eludes observation.

Actually Jolles argues for an oral *Sage*, which has no written
counterpart outside of Iceland. Since he has no written record for its
observation, he must conclude that such *Sagen* in Greece and
Germany recounted the tales of family life much as the Icelandic
Sagas did. His definition of the form depends completely on the

concept family. If one takes this concept away from the definition, Jolles has no way of distinguishing *Sage* from any other form.

Jolles's analysis moves to a level of abstraction which is useless in genre identification as the following example will illustrate. Jolles attempts to demonstrate the difference between the Throne Succession narratives and the patriarchal narratives:

> I refer only on the one hand to the events in the *Sage* of the patriarchs and, on the other to that which occurs in the house of David and what is being related in 2 Samuel and 1 Kings. Again we find comparable materials with quite different attitudes of mind and we realize that the form from which the patriarchs and their descendants derive is different from the form in which royal sons lived and were perceived during David's time. Here, the history of the family, the issue of the king, receive their interpretation from the view of the state of Israel.

The fundamental difference between the two is that the Throne Succession concerns itself with the question of the next king of Israel while the patriarchal narratives concern themselves with a family unrelated to a particular nation. The mere presence or absence of a king brings a change in genre identification.

Westermann takes up Jolles's three types of *Sage* and then argues, 'In the first and third group exact parallels obtain to the history of the patriarchs and the primeval history in Genesis'.[30] He then focuses on the patriarchal narratives and simply cites the definition of *Sage* given by Jolles. However, the term *Sage* itself has particular overtones which Westermann wishes to avoid on the following grounds:

> Unlike the Icelandic word Saga, the German word *Sage* has traditionally been so closely linked with the heroic tale that in German-speaking countries one immediately thinks of a saga of a hero when the word *Sage* is mentioned.[31]

Westermann has actually accepted the comparison between the Icelandic sagas and the biblical narratives, but rejects *Sage* on the basis of certain nuances of the German *Sage*.

Unfortunately Westermann's new term, family-tale (*Familien-Erzählung*), is a further abstraction upon Jolles's abstraction. We are caught in a language game, where genre terminology arises not out of literary analysis but out of a desire to avoid certain nuances connected with the term *Sage* in the German language. This can be of little help in the English-speaking world, where saga is defined as a distinct body of Icelandic literature.

The failure of the definition offered by Jolles and Westermann
shows up again when Westermann attempts to delineate the Joseph
cycle from the Abraham and Jacob-Esau cycles. As he must admit, all
three cyles deal with family relationships. However, the family
events reported in the Joseph cycle are more complicated than those
in the Abraham cycle since there we are not dealing simply with
father and son, but primarily with brother and brothers. This
complication of events corresponds to the complicated form of the
Novelle.[32] Westermann has added a second radical to the description
of *Sage* (*Familien-Erzählung*), that of complicated or uncomplicated
family events. Clearly, we cannot rely on these criteria for the
identification of one genre over against another.

III

Gunkel's definition of *Sage* arose out of his own observations of
narratives in Genesis. Jolles depended upon an analysis of Icelandic
saga but limited his definition to a consideration of content alone.
Westermann accepted Jolles's analysis but rejected the term *Sage*
because of its association with 'Heldensage' (hero tales). I would
suggest that we look again at the definition of saga as it relates to a
specific body of literature, namely the Icelandic sagas.

Saga in Icelandic simply means that which is said or told.
However, when the Icelanders began writing down oral narratives
which had existed for generations, they used the same term to apply
to the written record of those traditional stories as well. Thus the
term saga now applies to a distinct body of literature which arose in
Iceland from the tenth to the thirteenth centuries AD. The variety of
sagas is wider than that suggested by Jolles and includes 'riddara
sögur' (knights' tales) and 'lygi sögur' (lying tales). Nonetheless, we
may speak of a typical saga literature which includes the 'fornaldar
sögur', the kings' sagas, and the sagas of the Icelanders,[33] actually
the same three groups as recognized by Jolles. Scholes and Kellogg
use the term saga to apply in literary criticism to the Icelandic family
sagas, but this presupposes that the 'Islendiga sögur' formed the
model for the creation of the kings' sagas and the 'fornaldar' sagas.[34]
Nevertheless, a distinct body of literature exists for which the term
saga remains a meaningful designation. What are the characteristics
of that literature?

There are two schools of thought on the origin of the saga. Andreas

Huesler and Knut Liestöl contend that the sagas received their present form through a long period of oral tradition.[36] The storyteller or sagaman was primarily responsible for the form of the saga. The scribe did little more than to write down what was already fixed in oral tradition. In contrast to these free-prose theorists,[37] Nordal, Olsen, and Turville-Petre contend that the sagas are basically written compositions which depend upon oral tradition but receive their distinctive shape from an 'author'.[38] Turville-Petre goes so far as to say that 'the Family Sagas must be studied as the product of a literary movement . . .',[39] but even he is forced to admit that the sources of the sagas were oral tradition.[40] The disagreement in the debate centers on the definitive stage of the saga and not whether oral tradition lies behind the written sagas. Since no one disputes whether oral tradition lies behind the written record, Scholes and Kellogg suggest as one characteristic of saga, 'a traditional prose narrative'.[41] 'By "traditional" is meant narrative which bears the formal and rhetorical stigmata or oral composition.'[42] We may say that saga is written prose narrative which may bear the marks of oral prose composition.

Saga does not refer in literary criticism to an individual story but to a conglomerate of stories which normally center in a person or persons. W.P. Ker has given a classic description of the Icelandic saga:

> The original matter of the oral traditions, out of which the written Sagas were formed, was naturally very much made up of separate anecdotes, loosely strung together by associations with a district or family. Many of the Sagas are mere loose strings of adventures, of short stories, or idylls, which may easily be detached and remembered out of connection with the rest of the series.[43]

A saga is a narrative of greater duration than a single story and may be as long as a novel in length. Only one Icelandic saga reaches these proportions, namely Njala.

The sagas employ a brevity of style and the prose diverges greatly from the occasional scaldic verses which appear within them. 'If not the greatest charm of the Sagas, at any rate that which is perhaps most generally appreciated by modern readers is their economy of phrasing in the critical passages, the brevity with which the incidents and speeches are conveyed, the restriction of all commentary to the least available compass.'[44] We thus find few descriptive adjectives

because 'the prose is so plain, so completely non-lyric, that it does not even allow an occasional ornament adjective'.[45]
Einarsson summarizes the distinctive style and composition of the saga thus:

1. They name a great number of persons, and when a man 'is named in the story' or introduced, his genealogy is usually given and he may be described in a few words. The number of persons mentioned may vary from about six hundred in the saga of Njala with twenty-five main characters to twenty-four persons in the saga of Hranfnkatla with eight main characters.
2. The sagas are usually told in as much chronological order as possible: when two strands of the story coincide, the author must tell first one, then the others.
3. The sagas are written in a factual or matter of fact style, making the action swift, lucid, and dramatic. Apart from the weakness for genealogy and personal history, . . . the sagas are remarkable free from any digressions not absolutely essential to the story. Descriptions of nature are rare, occurring only as integral parts of the story. Psychological descriptions and moralizing harangues are conspicuous by their absence, likewise any kind of learned digressions.
4. One of the most marked characteristics of the sagas is the objective neutral point of view of their authors. The detached point of view made the saga-writer especially fine evaluators and describers of character . . . characters were mainly described by their acting and interacting upon other characters, . . . The method of description is always external, dramatic; thoughts are practically never revealed, except in speeches—and not always then.
5. One of the main charms of the sagas is precisely how much one can and must read there between the lines.[46]

Saga is a term used in literary criticism to describe narrative literature whose origins lie in oral prose composition and whose duration is greater than a single story. The individual stories or narratives are only loosely strung together by an association with a family or region so that it is next to impossible to uncover a plot. The narrators (authors) provide almost no narrative digression, with the result that characters are described primarily by their action. Sagas may include two or more versions of the same story but will tell them in as much chronological order as possible.

IV

The above definition of saga leads us to consider another question before we complete a comparison of the Icelandic saga with the Genesis material. Gunkel asked, 'What unit is really the constituent unit in Genesis, the one which we should first apply ourselves to?'[47] Gunkel, of course, argued that the individual story should first occupy the investigator.[48] If our answer is the same, saga, as it is used in reference to Icelandic literature, can have no meaning for our discipline. But it is precisely this presupposition which we must challenge. Should an individual story, as Gunkel presupposes, be interpreted first from within?

Gunkel cites in this connection Gen 16 as an example of a 'primitive narrative', which contains no antecedent assumptions.[49] However, when we investigate the story, we discover how difficult it is to analyze it from within. Gunkel suggests that the turning point of the narrative occurs in v. 6 when Hagar flees from the household of Abraham.[50] In v. 9 Hagar is told to return to her mistress. This command cannot be accounted for within the story, but occurs because of the necessity to have Ishmael back in the household of Abraham in order to explain the second expulsion of Hagar and her son in Gen 21.8ff. At an elementary level the investigator must have in mind the whole cycle of stories about Abraham in order to interpret what lies before us in Gen 16.

The preoccupation with the individual narrative has led to a fundamental misinterpretation of the story. Interpreters usually assume that the annunciation in vv. 11-12 belongs to the earliest story about the expulsion of Hagar and 'the birth of Ishmael'.[51] But, first, this immediately poses a problem because of the juxtaposition of the promise of numerous descendants (v. 10) and the annunciation (vv. 11-12). Secondly, the annunciation impedes the development of the story. Thirdly, the destiny of Ishmael which includes the plurality of his brothers (v. 12b) reflects the situation at the close of the 'Abraham cycle.' The annunciation in Gen. 16 proclaims the fate of Ishmael realized in Gen 25.1ff. We can conclude that the annunciation is an attempt to suggest to the listener (reader) a conclusion not realized in the scope of the immediate story but present in Gen 25.1ff.[52]

If one observes carefully, the narrative collapses after v. 6. Although we may wish to speak of a mixed narrative, as Gunkel does, a more accurate description would be that Gunkel's constitutive unit is irrecoverable in this case because of the relation of the story of Hagar's flight to the larger complex of tradition, the so called 'Abraham cycle'. The constitutive unit, 'the primitive story', is no longer in existence.

We may cite a second example which will help clarify the relationship between an individual story and the Abraham cycle. Here we will first attempt to define the 'constitutive unit' which lies behind Gen 18.9-16 and Gen 17.15-22.

The similarity of Gen 17 and 18 has been observed by von Rad, who notes that 17.15-22 'correspond basically (of course after extreme reduction to the theological) to the substance of ch. 18 (Sarah, subject of God's address, promise of a son, the laugh, the unbelieving question, the time "next year")'.[53] Our concerns go deeper than von Rad's comparison: we seek the common story which lies behind the two narratives.

Genesis 17.15 reports the renaming of Sarah—an 'external sign of an important turn in the life or function of the bearer'.[54] The implicit reason for the change in Sarah's name is God's promise of a son. Her life turns from barrenness and disgrace to fruitfulness and honor. In Gen 18.9 God asks Abraham, 'Where is Sarah your wife?' There is no preparation, no introduction, simply this question. These sudden references to Sarah are striking, but they serve to introduce the subject of the promise which immediately follows.[55]

In the next moment of the story God promises that Sarah will bear a child. The phrasing of the promise in Gen 17.16 approximates the style often found in P, whether it be God's gift of the land or the promise of numerous descendants.[56] The promise in Gen 18.10 states the exact time of birth.[57] Sarah is subject of God's promise in both accounts. Although the formulation of the promise varies, its intent does not.

In healing narratives healing may come through a miracle-working word,[58] a gesture or the laying on of hands,[59] through the power of a name,[60] or by a prescribed act.[61] In Gen 17 and 18 the narrative centers on the word which declares healing. Its prominence is shown by reiteration, by setting the counterpoint to laughter, and by introducing the goal toward which the narrative progresses. The assurance of healing is a formal element of healing narratives.

Hearing the promise, Sarah and Abraham laugh in the face of God. This has puzzled exegetes and has prompted several interpretations. Sarah's laughter has been explained psychologically,[62] etiologically (as a proleptic explanation of the name *yiṣḥāq*),[63] and theologically.[64] Abraham, on the other hand, appears to be in a different position since he knows with whom he is speaking. The absurdity of his laughter, particularly since it occurs in the Priestly account, has led to various attempts to circumvent this difficult theological construct: translating the verb *ṣḥq* as to smile[65] or rejoice,[66] questioning the authenticity of the passage,[67] psychologizing it,[68] or positing the necessity for explaining the name Isaac.[69] Can a satisfactory answer be provided from the narrative's structure and character?

The obvious reason for the laughter is the impossibility of child-bearing for Sarah. In Gen 18 Sarah is old (v. 11), her menses have stopped (v. 11), and she has never born a child (v. 12). The accent in Gen 17 falls upon the relative ages of Sarah and Abraham. Abraham questions the promise by asking, 'Shall a man a hundred years old sire a child or Sarah a woman of ninety give birth?' (v. 17).[70]

Derision directed to the one who proclaims healing is often a formal element in miracle narratives since the improbability of cure is cause for disbelief.[71] When the Shunammite woman responds to the promise of Elisha, she declares, 'Do not lie to your maidservant'.[72] When Naaman is told that he will be cured by bathing in the Jordan, he expresses indignation and disbelief.[73] Doubt of and contempt for the healer are frequently portrayed in healing stories.[74]

Therefore, the laughter of Sarah (Gen 18) and Abraham (Gen 17) should be understood as a formal part of the story. Laughter is the response of one who is confronted with what is deemed impossible— the birth of a child in old age. Neither psychologizing nor positing a need for the explanation of the name explains the prominence of this motif within the narrative. Its presence is due to the character of the story as a healing narrative.

Sarah's laughter is discovered by Yahweh, even though she is not visible to him (Gen 18.13). The reply, 'Is anything too wonderful for Yahweh?',[76] means that what is impossible with men is possible with God.[77] God's power is without limits. His discovery of Sarah's doubt is a concrete example of this power since from God nothing is hidden.[78] Sarah immediately becomes frightened because she knows with whom she speaks. The visitor is no ordinary man; she stands in the presence of the deity. The discovery of Sarah's laughter and the rhetorical question about the miraculous power of Yahweh confirm the story's basic character as a healing narrative.

After the laughter of Sarah in Gen 18, God reiterates the promise of a son (v. 14). Compared to the declaration in v. 10 the promise shows a certain freedom in its formulation.[79] Nevertheless, in each instance it consists of two clauses, one verbal and the other nominal, describing two simultaneous events: the return of Yahweh and the possession of a child by Sarah.[80] The promise declares that Sarah will possess a child within a specified time, 'at this time in a year'.[81] Although the promise appears in a relative clause in Gen 17.21b, its features correspond to those found in Gen 18.10, 14. The time of birth is indicated by *lammô'ēd hazzeh baššānâ hā'aḥeret*, where *baššānâ hā'aḥeret* is a circumlocution for *ḥayyâ*.[82] Sarah is subject of the promise granting her a son within a specified time. The similarity between this assurance and that found in Gen 18 is unmistakable.

The flexibility in the promise's expression suggests that we are not dealing with a fixed formula. Yet the style of the promise in Gen 18.10, 14 and 17.21b bears a close resemblance to healing predictions where the exact time of an event is foretold. Predictions of events within specified times occur in prophetic narratives of healing or threat.[83] An exact parallel is found in 2 Kgs 4.16f., where a prophet promises a son to a woman whose life has been marred by infertility and barrenness. The prominence of this motif is a further indication of the formal character of the story as a healing narrative.

With such an explicit reference to the times of birth (Gen 17.21b and 18.14), we would expect an account of that to be part of the narrative. Healing narratives, in which such predictions are made, invariably report the fulfillment of the prophetic word. The report of Isaac's birth in Gen 21.2 can be taken as an ending of the account in vv. 15-21 since, as Paul Humbert has shown, the language of this verse corresponds to the phrasing of the promise in 17.21b.[84] Gunkel recognized the necessity for the narrative in Gen 18 to report the birth of the child: 'In 10.14 (Gen 18) wird eine Fortsetzung der *Sage* angekündigt, die ursprünglich notwendig gefolgt sein muss . . . Diese Fortsetzung muss erzählen: wie sich die Verheissung erfüllte: wie Sara einen Sohn gebar . . .'.[85] Undoubtedly 21.1-2a is the conclusion of that narrative.

This accords with the ending usually present in healing narratives. The prophet speaks and the miracle is effected. In 2 Kgs 4.16 the prophet proclaims that a mother will embrace a child and the following verse reports the birth of a son. Elisha promised Naaman that he would be healed when he bathed in the Jordan. Naaman's leprosy was cured just as the prophet said (2 Kgs 5.14). The ending of the narrative with the child's birth—as promised by the deity—reflects the character of the healing narrative in the Old Testament.

We are reluctant to identify a narrative form only sparsely represented in the Old Testament because healing narratives are indeed rare within the prophetic traditions.[86] However, both narratives exhibit characteristics most commonly associated with healing or miracle stories.[87] Even the style of the promise approximates that found in healing narratives. The laughter at the promise of God is best explained by the usual presence of doubt in such stories. Finally, God's gift of fertility is a recurring theme throughout the Old Testament, e.g. Gen 25.21, 29.31 and 1 Sam 1.19f.[88] The narratives in Gen 17 and 18 are an exposition of this theme and a demonstration of God's power to bring birth long after the human faculties for such are past. The weight of evidence would appear to justify calling the stories, in Gen 17 and 18, healing narratives.

At the earliest level the purpose of the story was to glorify the God of Israel as the guarantor of fecundity. The child at this stage was a symbol, an expression of the divine power. The story emphasized the divine gift of fertility.

A parallel phenomenon is found in inscriptions from Epidauros which date from the third century BC. An inscription, partially effaced, presents the following cure:

> ... For the sake of children.
> She incubated and [had a dream.
> It appeared] that the [god] said
> she would have conception, and ...
> then she answered ... [from the] is
> she bore a son wi[thin a y]ear.[89]

Although the action of the god may differ within the dream revelation, the pattern of the report follows fixed lines. Generally the name and condition of the incubant are included in the account. When a woman is visited by Asklepios, the action or word of the god is an indication that her disease of infertility has been healed. Afterwards she bears a child, in most instances a boy. These reports are healing narratives as the title of the inscriptions suggests: 'Healing of Apollo and Asklepios'.[90] Whether the texts are understood as encouragement to those who entered the sanctuary or simply missionary propaganda, they demonstrate the healing power of Asklepios.

The healing narratives of Epidauros exhibit a form similar to those found in Gen 17 and 18. There is no interest in the son's name or destiny in a healing narrative, for the child is simply an expression of the divine power as, for example, in the healing narrative of 2 Kgs 4.11ff. The preceding analysis has shown that the story's early concern was the promise of a child and the divine gift of fertility. The issue of the miracle story was not who was born but that a child was born by the power of a divine promise.

The narratives in their present context are broken at the most decisive and climactic point, since they do not continue to tell of the birth of the child as promised by the deity but end abruptly in Gen 17.22 and 18.16. The reports of the child's birth are now gathered together in Gen 21.1-7 and identify a particular child, Isaac, Abraham's heir apparent. The individual stories serve the interest of the 'Abraham cycle' and cease to function as healing narratives, if indeed they ever existed as such independent entities. We have tried to show that these narratives must be examined as they function within the 'Abraham cycle'.

Gunkel supposed that when the narrator told the story orally he paused between each story, but when these stories were written down the pause disappeared so that the individual story, 'the constitutive unit', could be spoiled by its interrelationship with other stories. That pause, if it did occur, no longer occurs, with the result that the narratives exist in their interrelationship with other narratives. In this recognition, the investigator must begin with what is given, the narratives in their interrelationship with one another. We might therefore speak of 'The Saga of Abraham' or 'The Saga of Jacob'.

When the investigator begins at this level, he may take Gunkel's description of the Genesis narratives in the section of his commentary entitled 'Kunstform der Sagen', and interchange what he says there with what Einarsson and Ker say about Icelandic saga. In the Genesis narratives or in the Icelandic sagas we find little interest in nature, and economy of detail, the absence of narrative digression, the importance of the principal character, the conglomerate character of the interrelated narratives, the absence of plot, the description of character through action rather than word, the credibility of the story, the use of geneaology, and narrative composition of greater duration than a single story.

We have already observed that a mark of saga is oral prose composition. This runs counter to Gunkel's earlier thinking that the narratives may have existed in poetic form prior to their prose composition. The failure to uncover this earlier poetic form should push us to investigate the laws of oral prose composition as they may relate to the Genesis narratives. We should expect to find the marks of oral prose composition in the Genesis narratives, although we would suspect that the degree to which we can detect oral prose composition will be as debated in Old Testament study as it is in the study of Icelandic literature.

Saga is indeed a fitting category for the narrative material in Genesis. However, it should refer to what we have generally called the 'Sagenkranz' or saga cycle. We are suggesting that we refer to Gen 12.1–25.18 as 'The Saga of Abraham'.

2

THE MOSES NARRATIVES AS HEROIC SAGA

George W. Coats

1. *Introduction*

Moses is a problem. Modern historians and theologians would like to draw conclusions about his life's work, the office he may have held for his people, even the original form and content of the narratives that describe him. Was he a prophet, the first in a long line of charismatic prophets who spoke the Word of Yahweh?[1] Was he a covenant mediator, the go-between who made life before Yahweh possible for the chosen people?[2] Or perhaps he should be described as the founder of a great religion.[3] But conclusions are difficult to establish. The reason for the difficulty is, in part, the relative paucity of material, but in part also the character of the material available. For the historian the question is pressing: Was Moses originally a part of only one event now preserved within the overall structure of the Pentateuch?[4] Or did Moses do for the people of Israel essentially what the themes associated with his name say he did?[5]

Yet, in all of these questions a methodological problem lies hidden. Before the work of the historian or the theologian can be undertaken, the work of a literary critic must be completed. The tasks must not be confused. So, the initial question to pose to the Moses narratives is not what office or what dynasty, but what literature. Why did Israel remember Moses as it did? And how did its memory affect its story? If in an effort to speak to these questions some conclusions about the history of Israel in its earlier stages can be established, so much the better. But the first task is not a quest for the historical Moses.[6]

Martin Noth understood the necessity for such a methodological caveat. So, he prepared a foundation for his *History of Israel* by exploring, among other subjects, the tradition history of the

Pentateuch. The intention of his work was quite sound. In his work, however, he assumed from the beginning that the major structural divisions of the Pentateuch were independent of each other. His question about Moses fits consistently with the assumption: 'In which of the various Pentateuchal themes was the figure of Moses actually at home, from which only subsequently in the process of the merging of the Pentateuchal themes he came to dominate such a wide narrative sphere?'[7] That assumption is a problem in itself. But the procedure arises, so it seems to me, from an historian's concern to find the original Moses, and it fails to hear adequately the voice of the literature. It is not an adequate evaluation of the evidence, either for historical or for literary goals, to conclude that Moses was originally a part of the conquest theme.[8] The tradition about Moses' grave is strong. But it does not permit an essentially historical conclusion that Moses can be located in the general pattern of traditions about possession of the land.[9] How, then, can the Moses narratives be evaluated in a more satisfactory way? Ann Margaret Vater poses a series of questions that may avoid the hidden problem: 'What underlying or all-pervasive Moses image realizes, i.e., actualizes the roles or functions of history and tradition according to our witness? ... What are the narration patterns and other formal elements which carry the image? What is the narration use of those patterns and elements? And finally, what story do the patterns which carry the image tell?'[10]

2. *Working Hypothesis*

In order to meet these questions, I propose the following as a working hypothesis: *The Moses narratives can be understood, bracketed together, as heroic saga.*

a. *The thesis meets several initial problems.*
    1. Noth observed, in response to a suggestion that Moses serves as a great bracket binding all the 'themes' together: 'But in view of the factors just presented, would not Moses perhaps undermine the whole thesis that there are different Pentateuchal themes?'[11] In order to meet the suggestion, Noth must either show that Moses was not originally a part of all the themes (the patriarchs obviously falling out of consideration) or give up the thesis that the themes were originally independent.[12] Noth chose the former. The latter seems to

me necessary. Noth himself builds strong cases for concluding that Moses is closely bound with exodus, or wanderings, or Sinai. And he then rejects the cases. But his reasons for rejecting them are not always so strong. One illustration will demonstrate the point! Noth dismisses Moses from the exodus theme in part because the birth and abandonment tale is 'one of the latest and most secondary passages of the Moses tradition'. That it has a narrative motif known all over the world is not evidence that it is literarily secondary. That it does not mesh well with the oppression theme and thus the vocation-plague cycle may perhaps provide such evidence.[13] And yet the distinctive role of such Moses traditions as this one, the Midianite marriage, the battle with Amalek, or the humble image (Num 12) must not be overlooked. On the basis of this observation, I would reformulate the hypothesis: *The Moses narratives, structured as heroic saga, merge with narrative tradition about Yahweh's mighty acts, structured around confessional themes*. These two structural models stand as narrative opposites, at times complementary, at times contradictory. They find their largest expression in the structural opposition represented by the Pentateuch/Hexateuch debate.

2.   Bernhard Anderson asserts: 'The exodus story is not a heroic epic told to celebrate the accomplishment of Moses as the liberator of his people'.[14] The issue here is not over the terms 'saga' or 'epic'. Rather the problem turns on the designation of the story as 'heroic'. In order to speak to the issue, first, it is necessary to establish some definition of 'heroic' as an interpretative tool. Joseph Campbell proposes one description: 'A hero ventures forth from the world of common day into a region of supernatural wonder: fabulous forces are encountered and a decisive victory is won: the hero comes back from this mysterious adventure with the power to bestow boons on his fellow man'.[15] The parallel with Moses is apparent. Thus I would expand the working hypothesis. For this heroic saga, I would emphasize the characteristic trait in heroic tradition that binds the hero to his people, his fellow creatures. Either by military might or by skillful intercession, he defends his own. He brings 'boons' to his company. But second, some probe of Anderson's objection is in order. His position is primarily theological, not literary-critical. He continues: 'The exodus story is not . . . told to celebrate the accomplishment of Moses . . . The narrator's major purpose is to glorify the God of Israel, the "Divine Warrior" whose strong hand and outstretched arm won the victory over his adversaries.'[16] The

objection thus assumes a contradiction between the intentions to glorify God and to celebrate the deeds of Moses. The story may be one or the other but not both. This position is, however, an unproven assumption. It is my conviction that the two may stand together. Indeed, the intertwining of the two can be expressed in terms of literary structure by the revised hypothesis: *The Moses heroic saga, the narrative of Moses for his own people, merges with a narrative structure built around the mighty acts of God.*

3. John van Seters argues that the term 'saga' is inadequate for current Old Testament debate and should be dropped. The primary reasons for his objections derive from a solid critique of the use various form critics have made of the term in the past decades.[17] It does not follow, however, that the term has no currency for current studies in Old Testament narrative. A more workable definition for saga suggests that as an analytic term for a narrative genre, it refers to a long prose narration, usually episodic in character, built around a plot or a succession of plots. This designation of genre seems to me to be preferable to biography.[18] It is true that in the ancient world, biography was as much a literary construct as it was a work of history. 'Most Greek biographers were less concerned with presenting historical facts and detailed accounts than with presenting a clearly defined character, though Plutarch ... gives not mere eulogies but abundant concrete details about illustrious Greeks and Romans.'[19] Thus, the description of biography shows close contact with the description of the genre under consideration here. It seems to me to be clear, however, that 'biography' carries more freight for historical detail than is consistent with the Moses tradition. 'The modern view of biography as the accurately detailed history of a man, with attention paid not only to his deeds but to his thoughts and his environment',[20] suggests a genre quite distinct from the Moses tradition. It is that difference that 'heroic saga' connotes. Heroic saga does not chronicle the events in the life of the central figure. Rather, it projects an image of the hero as the defender of his people. Its intention is to capture its audience by the tensions in its story-line, thus, to entertain its audience with the skill of its storytelling, although it would have been quite possible to transcribe the substance of the story-line at some point in its history. The episodic structure would enable the storyteller to create his story with each performance by skillfully constructing the panels or episodes to fit his need. But the episodes would follow a typical, perhaps even a set, pattern.

b. *The structure of heroic saga*

1. Heroic narrative typically enframes its story with some account of the hero's birth and death. That the J account of Moses' death is heroic has previously been suggested.[21] That his birth and adoption into the royal Egyptian court should be considered heroic is also not new, although it has not been explored in detail under a heroic rubric.[22] Heroic motifs include not only the threat to his life by the pogrom, with the corresponding exposure that commits him to his fate, but also the irony that develops in the princess's decision to commit him to a Hebrew mother for his initial nurture. How could he do anything other than identify with his own people?

In addition to the birth–death frame, several distinct story units reflect a heroic cast. In Exod 2.11-22, Moses reveals his character. This point appears first in his decision, while virtually a prince in the Pharaoh's house, to commit himself to his people. Indeed, it is this explicit commitment to the people that establishes a leitmotif for the Moses heroic saga. But the heroic quality of Moses appears not only in the unique commitment to his people, but also in the typical intervention he displays, first for one of his brothers, then for a group of helpless women. The heroic quality is apparent, however, not simply in his defense of the defenseless, but in (1) his display of physical strength leading finally to his marriage, and (2) his flight to a foreign land, away from his own people.[23] It is significant incidentally that both the birth-adoption tale and the marriage tale belong to J. P's announcement of Moses' death in Num 27.12-23, now converted to an appeal for a successor, must have originally reported the event as well. But it is remarkably unheroic in its presentation (see also Deut 31.1-2). And P eschews any reference at all to the birth or marriage.

In addition to these story units, other episodes in the wilderness traditions seem more closely bound to Moses than to the thematic structure emphasizing God's leadership. (1) Mosaic legends can be seen in Exod 17.8-16[24] and Num 12.[25] (2) Exod 18 intends in its present form, the work of E or perhaps a JE redaction, to show a proper decentralization of the Mosaic judicial office. But the organization scheme is now attached to an account of Moses' meeting with Jethro. The account may undergird a tradition of covenant bond between Jethro and Moses.[26] But it also reveals a description of Moses as storyteller, a heroic motif. Indeed, the merged structures complement each other at just this point. For Moses the storyteller tells his story about Yahweh. The account he relates must be in some manner a feather in his own bonnet. But its focus falls on the mighty acts of God that brought Moses and his people so far into the wilderness.

2.   It seems to be clear, then, that for J or JE a major part of the heroic saga builds on Mosaic tradition associated with Midian. A crucial linchpin in the argument for the hypothesis would thus be developed by probing the vocation account in J (Exod 3.1–4.23) as a contrast to the one in P (Exod 6.2–7.6). The goal of the probe would not be to determine whether the tradition originally set the events described in Midian or in Egypt, or even whether the call originally commissioned Moses to go to the Pharaoh or the elders of Israel. It is not in the first order a traditio-historical probe. The goal is rather to penetrate the character of the narrative.

The general form-critical pattern of the narrative has been explored in sufficient detail.[27] I would open the probe, then, with some detailed examination of the commission. (1) From the beginning the narrative depicts a personal address to Moses. This point is established, not simply by the speech formulas that note when a speech of Yahweh is addressed to Moses. It is a part of the dialogue, the opening double vocative which honors Moses by name, *Mosheh, Mosheh.* The commission itself, vv. 7-12, begins without reference to Moses. Yahweh reports his experience: 'I have seen the affliction of *my* people . . . I have heard their cry . . . I know their suffering.' And then he announces his intentions: 'I have come down to deliver them . . . ' There is no personal address here. Moses is virtually a vessel for Yahweh's message. The pattern shifts, however, in v. 9. It would appear almost as if the address is to be duplicated. 'The cry of the people of Israel has come to me . . . I have seen the oppression . . .' But the opening is followed, not by an announcement of divine intention, but by a personal commission: 'Come, I will send *you* to Pharaoh'. Moreover, the purpose of the commission does not cast Moses as a vessel. To the contrary, Moses will be actively an agent in the redemptive event: 'That *you* may bring forth my people'. The duplication thus does not reflect a composition out of two sources but the merging of two tradition structures.

3.   In the renewed commission, vv. 16-17, a new motif appears. Moses is to go first to the elders of Israel. And only when they have been convinced will he go with the elders to the Pharaoh. The announcement is that Yahweh will save. But the response orients to

Moses: 'They will harken to *your* voice'. The important motif here, however, is the movement of Moses, not as a lone eagle, but with his people, with their representatives. Moses' stature develops only as his commission develops for his fellow Hebrews.

4. The objections also have a role to play in heroic structure.[28] The hero accepts his role for his people with reluctance. And Yahweh responds with a promise for his presence. Even the *idem per idem* formula in v. 14 functions, on the basis of a word play with v. 12, as a promise for divine presence. The verse suggests, moreover, that Yahweh's very name is a sign to guarantee the promise. The following announcement of worship on the mountain is closely connected to the sign, a result of the presence.[29] It suggests that worship on the mountain of God will be possible only by virtue of God's promise to be present with his people. But there is a more important function of the sign. Verse 12 shows the promise for the sign to be directed to Moses personally (cf. the second person *singular* suffixes). Moreover, the sign confirms the authority of the commission. And on the basis of the sign, *Moses*, not Yahweh, will bring the people out of Egypt. The completion of the sign in the worship involves all the people (cf. the second person *plural* verb form). And the worship will be directed to God. But still, the sign qualifies Moses' position. It enables the people to believe in him. And so the pattern of the commission is completed.

The sign, however, continues as a motif in the narrative development. In 4.1-9 a new series of signs appears. It functions nevertheless as the name does to confirm the authority of both the sender and the sent. Indeed, the series is oriented first to the elders of the people. And the goal is to secure their belief in the commission. The signs would apparently function in the same way for the Pharaoh (cf. 3.20; 4.21). For J this point appears not only in 4.21-23, a section which may be secondary and derived from the plague cycle, but also in the plague cycle itself. The cycle would in fact not be a distinct and independent narrative, but the proper continuation of the vocation account, connected on the basis of the typical commission-execution pattern noted throughout Pentateuchal narratives. The function of the sign for confirming the authority for both Moses and Yahweh is apparent in the Pharaoh's confession (10.16), where he admits that his hard heart has been a sin against both Yahweh and Moses. The combination would perhaps point to the merged structures suggested by the working hypothesis.

Moreover, the power to accomplish such signs, obviously residing in Yahweh's hands, has been given to Moses (4.21). It now becomes a part of his portfolio as the leader of the people. Even the rod belongs in a very personal way to Moses (4.17).[30] This assertion is not contradicted by the introduction of Aaron in Exod 4.10-16 and 27-31, a section which may be secondary in the overall narrative tradition.[31] To be sure, because Moses angers Yahweh with his objection excuse, Aaron is also commissioned. And the privilege to do signs is passed to him (v. 30). But the power and authority represented by the signs resides still in Moses, through God's ordination (v. 28). Indeed, Moses stands as God for Aaron.

One final point is necessary for the analysis of J's vocation account. The negotiations symbolized by the signs end in failure (10.28-29). But this point does not upset the heroic image. To the contrary, what Moses could not win by open negotiation he wins by cunning. His cunning skill is depicted for the narrative by the spoil and secret escape, a description of the exodus now reduced to fragments by the death of the first-born.[32] It is nonetheless important for the image of the heroic Moses not only because of the leadership it represents, but also because of the description of Moses it builds on (11.3b).

The vocation tradition and its extension into the plague cycle thus give witness to the intention of Yahweh to save his people from the oppression of the Pharaoh. But it also reveals a marked elevation of Moses. The signs he does and the rod he carries serve as seals for the great authority associated with his name. It is that elevation, that reverence and authority, which mark the narrative as a whole as heroic.

5.   In contrast to J the P vocation account and its extension into the plague cycle is markedly unheroic. The narrative begins in 6.2 as if it were *in medias res*. There is no personal vocative, no commission for Moses to do anything. To the contrary there is only instruction for a speech. The speech contains an announcement of Yahweh's intention to save his people. But it provokes no positive response from the people, no commitment to Moses. There is a second speech, a second command to deliver a message. But again, there is no invitation to Moses to participate in the act. That point does not appear until v. 13. And at that point the charge, involving both Moses and Aaron equally (cf. v. 26), is in all probability secondary, a reduplication bridge used for incorporating the Aaronic genealogy in vv. 14-25. The P account also contains the designation of Moses as

God. But the description is shifted. It no longer serves to subordinate Aaron, as it did in J. Here Moses is like God to the Pharaoh. And Aaron serves as his prophet. Moreover, there is no rod, no series of signs given to Moses. The signs here belong only to God. They show only God's authority. Moses would seem much more directly an instrument in the hands of God than a heroic figure who shares the faithful belief of the people with the deity.

6. The traditions of the wilderness wanderings present a similar heroic image. Indeed, the acts of benefit for the sake of the people serve not only to save the people in the face of crisis but to establish the authority of the leader as well. This point is most clearly expressed in Exod 14. In the face of crisis provoked by the Egyptian chariotry, Moses appeals to Yahweh but then leads his people out of danger. The military character of the tradition gives a prominent heroic cast to the material. But at the same time it shows Moses' heroic stand against the enemy, for the people. The event concludes with a notation that Israel believed in Yahweh and at the same time they believed in Moses (v. 31).[33] This is precisely the combination which lies at the foundation of the working hypothesis.

3. *Setting*

The problems posed by the Moses traditions are highlighted when one considers questions about setting. Childs poses the questions well, particularly regarding the tradition about Moses' vocation: 'Does the fixed form reflect the function of a particular institution or office which has shaped the material?'[34] His answer is rather subtle: 'The evidence points more convincingly toward seeing the setting of Ex 3 in the prophetic office'.[35] He does not suggest by that point that the Moses traditions were used as a foundation for the form of prophetism that developed in the monarchical period. There is no quasi-historical movement here which attempts to discover the original office Moses occupied. Rather, he sees a mutual influence between the Moses traditions and the later prophets: 'Particularly in the expanded form of the present text, the series of questions raised by Moses in objection to being sent echo the inner and outer struggles of the prophets of Israel'.[36] The mutual influence is clear. One has to consider only Deut 34.10 to see the impact of that influence. Yet, to define the setting for the text as 'prophetic office' may obscure the character of the influence. Perhaps both the Moses

vocation account and those of the prophets were influenced by a
third source. At least a brief look at Num 12.6-8 shows that some of
the influence from prophets on the Mosaic narrative was negative.
Childs sharpens the issue for the Moses traditions generally in his
treatment of the Mosaic office and Sinai. His suggestion in brief is
that two forms of the Mosaic office appear: 'In the E form of the
tradition Moses functioned as the covenant mediator and sealed the
covenant with Israel on the basis of the laws which he communicated
to the people (24.3). But in the J form . . . Moses functions as a
continual vehicle of the will of God in his office before the tent of
meeting.'[37] The stories do indeed depict Moses standing in the
breach between people and God. They show him in the tent of
meeting for the responsibilities of intercession. Yet, do these images
reflect an institutional setting? Do they suggest that the Moses
traditions were influenced by the on-going offices of covenant
mediator or intercessor? Or do they derive from the repertoire of
images available to the storyteller for depicting heroic patterns? Is
the growth of the Mosaic narrative not much more diffuse than
would be suggested by attaching it to one or the other institutional
setting? In that case both the Moses vocation account and the
prophetic reports of inner and outer struggle would show the
influence of heroic patterns, a typical manner available for depicting
such struggles! The frequentative form of verbs would show, not so
much institutional offices, but patterns of typical behavior for the
one man.

This point is perhaps clearest in Exod 32–34. Moses meets a
challenge that develops into near tragedy. When he leaves his people
for a short time, they seek a new leader. And the covenant is broken.
Moses' authority is rejected. But Moses refuses any honor that does
not include his people. And the entire unit unfolds around his
audacious intercession before God. His goal is immediate relationship between all the people and God. The imagery for this relationship draws on the motif of divine presence. God secures his presence
to Moses. But Moses wants more. And to that end he presses his
intercession. There is no covenant mediator here. To be sure, Moses
mediates the covenant. But the incident reflects the typical work of
the unique man. The movement of the narrative runs by any
permanent arrangement for building a covenant with the people
through Moses. It thus does not suggest a permanent office of
covenant mediator.

The same point applies for the shining face. 34.29-35 reflects something typical for Moses. But at the same time, it highlights the unique position this Moses holds for his people. The shining face and then the veil function as symbols for the authority of Moses. They even point to the intercessory role of the man. But they do not yet support the notion that an intercessory or prophetic office resides in the image. They point rather to the stature of the hero.[38]

The question of setting thus cannot easily be answered in terms of an institutional office. It presses much more toward a literary process, although the literary process may well belong to an oral frame of tradition. It suggests influence from the concerns of the storyteller. Moreover, it is clear that the storyteller looked at Moses in a very particular way. The underlying Moses image throughout the tradition, the image that actualizes the role of Moses for society in cultic or prophetic institutions, is *heroic*, the unique leader whose typical acts actualize the people. And the pattern of the hero carries the story forward. It is, indeed, the power of the story about the hero for his people that enables the people to live from the Mosaic context.

4. *Intention*

It seems to be clear, then, that the Moses narratives properly understood should be bracketed together as heroic saga, not separated among originally distinct and independent segments of narrative about Israel's early life. Moreover, these traditions intend to say that God redeemed Israel from bondage and led it through a hostile wilderness. That was God's act of salvation. But the same traditions also say that God's leadership was carried out by the heroic leadership of the man Moses. God saved Israel from the oppression of the Egyptians. But in fact it was Moses, the man who had stature in the eyes of the Egyptians, who carried out God's redemption in the day to day struggle with the Pharaoh. God led Israel through the wilderness, met the problems posed by hunger, thirst, and enemies, and deposited his people on the banks of the Jordan. But it was Moses (and Aaron) who met the day to day struggle with the wilderness and defended his people against physical want, pressure from wilderness enemies, and even the wrath of God himself. The intention of the tradition is not always to say that all leaders should be like Moses, although on occasion that might be the case (Exod 17; Num 12). The intention is to depict the founder of the people in an entertaining way but also in a way that glorifies not only God but also the hero who lived and died for his own. It is to say, with a certain kind of humble pride, that this man was the father of our people. Such a story is the content for saga.

3

LEGEND*

Ronald M. Hals

The field of OT form-critical terminology is one in which there exists great diversity and greater confusion. Each of us becomes painfully aware of both the diversity and the confusion in those particular areas in which he works. However, since each of us concentrates on different areas, the subject of form-critical terminology in general is almost never treated. While probably no researcher can treat the whole of this field, it is still vital that something be done lest troubles in our usage increase to the point where communication is no longer effective. It is my conviction that the difficulties which arise in dealing with terminology in one genre are likely to be related to those encountered in treating others, and thus one possible way to encourage reflection on the larger terminological issue would be to treat one area as a sample. If it can be traced how confusing usages have developed and why they remain in writing about one genre, such an investigation can have heuristic value for recognizing related problems elsewhere. Similarly, if a particular set of suggestions seems to be prompted by reflecting on the history and scope of usage in one category, it can be hoped that this may stimulate parallel suggestions at least in related categories. It is in this spirit that I have chosen to deal with legend as one sample area, hoping that the difficulties and prospects encountered here will be sufficiently typical to encourage others to write about their own areas.

I

In many ways dealing with legend can be a kind of 'fun thing'. For example, examining the definitions of legend put forth in standard reference works enables one to discover easily that the greats and

near-greats of both past and present could come up with some
surprisingly inadequate formulations. At first it seems attractive to
be able to point out the weaknesses of Gunkel, Gressmann, and
Mowinckel. It is only when one attempts to provide a more adequate
formulation that the pleasure departs and the pain begins. I do not
presume here to present the truly adequate definition of a legend. I
shall confine myself to setting forth some of the inadequacies in past
formulations, trying to indicate where possible the reasons behind
these inadequacies, and a brief glance at the present situation in
terminological usage with some future possibilities.

The first tip-off that one gets about the difficulty of the term
legend is the discovery that in many handbooks it is combined with
saga. This was already the case in the first edition of RGG,[1] and it
still prevails in Fohrer's *Introduction to the Old Testament*.[2] Usually
a separation of the two categories is undertaken at the beginning of
such combined treatments, but the shallowness of the separation is
often truly overwhelming. For example, Fohrer labels the legend
'only a special form of the former [saga], referring to persons and
places, periods and institutions, that are religiously significant or
sacred'.[3] One can only wonder which religiously *in*significant
persons, places, periods, and institutions are available to form the
subject matter of OT sagas! Eissfeldt makes virtually the same
distinction between saga and legend, observing that, 'if the men or
places or occasions which are central to the narrative are of religious
significance—priests or prophets, sanctuaries or festivals—then we
call such a narrative a legend'.[4] Here 'religious significance' is
implicitly defined by the examples mentioned, but surely this definition
cries out for protest. As Bentzen pointed out, to be convincing such a
'distinction must be founded upon purely formal, stylistic criteria',[5]
and to create a separate category because of a purely content-based
criterion seems unnecessary. It would indeed be unnecessary, if
legends were only a group of sagas dealing with priests or prophets
and sanctuaries or festivals instead of patriarchs and their family
matters, having no truly formal distinctiveness. However, if, as will
be contended here, the situation with regard to the meaning and use
of legend is more complicated, our investigation must be pushed
further.

It might be expected that Bentzen, in the light of his criticism of
improperly based distinctions, might have a more solid definition of
legend to offer. But surprisingly Bentzen goes on that it is character-

istic of a legend that 'it makes *propaganda* for some religious opinion or form of life', affirming that this is never the case with a saga (*sagn* in his terminology).[6] Regardless of the truth or falsity of this claim, the key phrase, '*propaganda* for some religious opinion', is impossibly imprecise, and we still lack an effective definition.

Even the old master Gunkel does not come off too well when he tries to define legend as the label appropriate to that type of narrative which developed in later years out of the older saga. For him this development can only be seen as degeneration. Both aesthetically and theologically legends, along with the Priestly Code and the Chronicles, reflect an unpleasant loss of the vigor and power of the past. Especially interesting is the place the hero occupies in Gunkel's analysis. For him only the old saga could portray a man as a hero, for 'the legend celebrates God alone'.[7] To me it seems obvious that in this analysis Gunkel's romanticism has come heavily to the fore,[8] rather than his usual form-critical insight.

Gressman had an opinion much similar to Gunkel's, feeling that the legends were artistically lacking, and linking this to the prominent place of miracles in legends. In contrast, though, Gressman could speak of legends as presenting heroes, 'spiritual heroes who have been active for the cause of religion and through their faith, life, and sufferings stand out exceptionally'. Perhaps a small difference between Gressman and Gunkel is also to be found in Gressman's statement that 'because these men stand in an especially close relationship to the deity, they are in a position to achieve more than ordinary men'.[9] This last difference, though, seems more a matter of formulation than content. In any case, this brief survey of definitions makes it amply clear that an area of terminological confusion does exist in the case of legend.

II

While this confusion about what a legend is seems bad enough, the matter is severely compounded when the problem of translation from one modern language to another is introduced. The German 'sage' is quite often rendered in English as 'legend', the translation of Gunkel's introduction to *Genesis*[10] as *Legends of Genesis*[11] being a good case in point. In the second edition of his *Understanding the Old Testament* Bernhard W. Anderson[12] refers to Albright's introduction[13] to the reprint of Gunkel's work in which the translational switch is pointed out, but in the index to Anderson's own book the entry 'legend' simply reads, 'see saga'.[14] Perhaps misled by such English usages, Bentzen affirms in a footnote that 'the *Danish* and *German* terms "*sagn*" and "*Sage*" and "*Legende*" as *English* equivalent have only one word: "*Legend*"'.[15] As a counsel of despair, Bentzen goes on to explain that he uses 'the *English* "*legend*" in the meaning of *Danish* "*sagn*"'.[16] For the Danish *Legende* he uses the term '"*devotional*" or "*edificatory legend*"'.[17] Thus we are now confronted by the specter of never being certain when we see the word legend in English what may lie behind it. The matter of Bentzen's added adjective is not at all helpful, since most writers affirm that a legend normally had an edifying intent. It is discouraging that Klaus Koch should have chosen in *The Growth of the Biblical Tradition* to affirm Bentzen's statement about the meaning of the English term legend, saying, 'the English *legend* has a wider meaning, and includes that of the German saga. The German term *legend* corresponds to the *devotional legend* or *edificatory legend*'.[18] It is easy to visualize the impossible task then confronting the translator of Koch's book, and he is perhaps not to be blamed severely for disregarding the footnote about the meaning of the English term legend, following simply the procedure of rendering *Sage* with the English saga and *Legende* with the English legend.

The point of all this is not merely to create sympathy for the task of a translator, although such sympathy is no doubt richly deserved. Rather, it is just at this point that we are brought to the threshold of new insight into the problem. When the question of translating form-critical terms from one language to another is examined, strange things are often discovered, and this is particularly true in the case of the term legend. Actually, it is precisely at this point that we can discover both the reasons for some of the present confusion and some guidelines for future policy. To me it seems that the basic reason for the confusion in the use of the terms saga and legend *in English* today can be discovered as soon as one broadens the scope of investigation from the noun to the adjective. Since the use of the term saga in English to render the German 'Sage' has become increasingly common in recent years, it seems at first glance unintelligible why translators should fluctuate so between the use of saga and legend. But when one goes on to consider the adjectives *sagenhaft* and *legendenhaft*, one confronts the fact that English provides no adjective from saga to correspond to legendary from legend. While it might be

possible to formulate such a word as 'saga-style', this seems not to
have happened. Instead repeatedly both 'sagenhaft' and 'legendenhaft'
are rendered in English translations with the one term legendary.

Further and more valuable insights occur when we ask the
question about what underlies the German word *Legende*. It is, of
course, derived from the Latin word *legenda* (originally neuter
plural) 'things to be read', used in medieval times to denote the
stories about holy men read on specified occasions. From this
beginning there came about a development according to which each
saint was assigned a particular day in the calendar and the story
about him was the appointed 'legend' (*legenda*, now feminine singular)
for that day. Beginning here Andre Jolles[19] undertook a rather
thorough investigation of the nature of this literary form in which he
classified it as 'a virtue embodied in a deed' (*tätige Tugend*).
Examining the mental process (*Geistesbeschäftigung*) involved led
him to conclude that the decisive element in a legend is that of the
imitabile or 'go and do likewise'.

In the light of this, two seemingly unrelated problems in the use of
legend as a form-critical label can now be understood as flowing from
the same cause. The fondness on the part of many writers for
distinguishing legend from saga on the ground that legend deals with
sacred persons can be understood, because saints are the normal
subject matter of medieval legends, and these legends are still used in
certain circles today. At the same time, the puzzling way in which
cultic 'legends' are so labeled now also makes sense. It is not because
these cultic legends deal with sacred places and are therefore to be
classified together with narratives dealing with sacred persons.
Rather it is because the story of the founding of a sanctuary is the
narrative which is naturally the one to be read at that sanctuary. But
this involves an entirely different use of the term *legendum*. The story
about the founding of a shrine, or for that matter the story about the
beginning of a ritual custom, is not necessarily at all a story about a
holy man whose behavior is to be imitated. In fact, it is entirely
possible that the story of the founding of a particular sanctuary could
be either entirely mythological or entirely historical. Its literary form
then might be that of myth or historiography, and thus the fact that it
was a narrative to be read at a particular sanctuary might have little
or nothing to do with its literary form or genre. Thus we have a form-
critical label which is basically unrelated to literary form. For
instance, the narrative to be read on one particular day in the ritual

calendar, i.e. the *legendum* for that day,[20] could be one of a number of possible literary types. On New Year's Day in Babylon one might read a myth, dealing with the warfare of the gods, while in Israel one might read from Genesis 1, an account so demythologized that it has lost both the plurality of gods and the element of dramatic suspense characteristic of myths. To bring the matter up to date, the fact that one reads the Gospel narrative of the circumcision of Christ on New Year's Day, while it makes this pericope the *legendum* for that day, does not at all imply any element of 'go and do likewise'. So, to speak of a New Year's Day legend is, by virtue of this ambiguity in the term legend, to open the door to misunderstanding.

III

Where then do we go from here? Undoubtedly the ideal direction in which to move would be toward a usage in which a given term would have the same meaning in every discipline, including such diverse fields of study as cultural anthropology and classical studies, not to mention the obviously related areas of Near Eastern studies, church history, and theology. How to accomplish movement in such a direction is another question. Since the work of Andre Jolles has been of such help,[21] it might seem that the handbooks of the more secular disciplines might offer us help in coming to generally accepted cross-disciplinary definitions. Although my investigations here have not been extensive, they have not met with any success beyond that referred to in connection with the work of Jolles. Consider, for example, the words of Douglas G. Haring, professor of anthropology at Syracuse University. He begins very broadly by characterizing as legend 'any nonhistorical story supposedly of ancient origin and unverifiable as history'.[22] Apparently feeling that even this broad description was not all-embracing enough, he goes on to state, 'nevertheless, the significance of the word is vague, and students of myth, folklore, and tradition have not assigned a precise generally accepted meaning to it . . . ',[23] thus not referring to the treatment of Jolles. More frightening, in view of its massive contradicting of the article's initial description, is the following: 'Popularly, there is a tendency to confuse legend with history and to accord undeserved credence to legendary materials. When a legend can be verified, however, it is accepted as history.'[24] The situation is not better when

Haring endeavors to distinguish between the related labels legend and myth:

> Legend also differs from myth, in that myths embody and symbolize the values for social and moral standards of the people who relate them. There need be nothing sacred about the legend in the modern sense; often it is merely a good story, while myths tell of divine beings and culture heroes and thus dramatize standards of conduct, at least by implication.[25]

What value, I wonder, can there be in a comparison which compares only 'legend in the modern sense' and myth in the classic sense?

IV

It seems to me that the confusion in usage of form-critical labels has progressed to such an extent that it must be asked whether in some cases any standardly acceptable technical terminology is salvable. While in the case of the term myth any uniformity seems beyond achievement, perhaps the situation has not yet progressed so far in the case of legend. It may just still be possible to limit the term legend to those narratives which in Jolles' formulation express 'a virtue embodied in a deed', and focus on the element of the *imitabile*. Such narrowing of the use of legend is not primarily suggested by the historical observation that this is how the term was originally employed as a label for a literary type. Rather, the major advantage is that here we have a single, specific variety of literature whose setting and mental process are relatively clear—in other words here we have a genre. To employ the label legend where only a minor aspect of the mental process involved in the *imitabile* is present is to use the label in an inappropriately broad way. Most legends of the saints tell of miraculous deeds, but some do not. The element of the miraculous is not essential to the genre legend, and this element is also common to other genres, such as myth and saga. A focus on sacred persons, places, times or institutions may well be characteristic of many legends, but it is not distinctively or exclusively so.

But then do we not come out with a neatly precise genre which is inapplicable to OT material? No, legends in Jolles's use of the term do occur in the OT. The stories in the first half of the book of Daniel are a case in point. They portray the virtue of fidelity embodied in a variety of deeds, and they clearly focus on the call to 'go and do likewise'. This truth is often pointed out in handbooks, although the situation is many times needlessly complicated by the addition of an adjective, both unnecessary and at times inaccurate, with the introduction of the term 'martyr legend'.[26]

It may already be too late to achieve such standardization, especially when one examines a treatment such as that of Mowinckel in *IDB*.[27] For Mowinckel the 'legend proper', as the *sagn* 'with edifying, devotional tendency, a story from the life and works of some religious hero, a saint, a prophet, an ancestor and culture hero', may be a myth or a historical narrative. This is not just a matter of my conclusion of what Mowinckel's usage might lead to, but his own express statement.

> As the cult *aition*, the legend is told at the festivals of the sanctuary with which the saint is connected. By definition even the legend may include a historical nucleus, as in the Moses and Exodus stories in their present form. Here the 'salvatory deeds', not of Moses, but of the Lord, are retold and re-experienced, and we may therefore call them the myth of the cultic feast.[28]

Here we witness in sharpest form the consequent confusion which results from the two-fold background of the term legend: first in the sense of *legendum*, as the narrative to be read on a particular occasion, and then in the sense of *legenda* (fem. sing.), as that particular type of narrative which came to be associated with the particular day of a saint.

If any standardization is to be achieved, it will not be enough simply to confine the use of the term legend to the type found in the first half of the book of Daniel. A substitute must also be found for the way legend has previously been used in these other contexts. Mowinckel's alternate term, the cult *aition*, is a possibility, but a more natural and widely used possibility is the other Greek term, *hieros logos*. This would do well enough for those cultic 'legends' such as the Bethel narrative in Gen 28.10ff., but a label must also be found for *legendum* in the sense of that narrative which is 'to be read'. My colleagues in the field of liturgics tell me that we may be just in time to take up the traditional term lection. While this term will endure in liturgical circles in the word lectionary and in Latin usage, it is about to be replaced in ecumenical circles with the simple word 'reading'. The other possible terms which suggest themselves here seem to me to be less suitable for a variety of reasons. 'Pericope' seems more to suggest simply a literary unit, whether ever designated to be read in some ritual cycle or not. The term 'lesson' has a firm background in some liturgical circles, but runs the risk of being misunderstood as implying a didactic emphasis by those who do not share this liturgical background. It could perhaps be rescued by the addition of the adjective 'appointed', but it seems best wherever possible to avoid the use of such qualificatory adjectives in genre labels.

The only remaining prominent difficulty is that use of the term legend in connection with the literary type often called the prophet legend. Klaus Koch adopts this usage,[29] although many German writers simply use the labels *Prophetengeschichte* or *Prophetenerzählung* which are then rendered into English as prophet story.[30] Koch is thoroughly aware both of the essential nature of a legend as pointed out by Jolles and of the differentness of the OT narratives about the prophets, but still he feels that legend is the best term.

> There is obviously a sharp difference between the medieval legend and the Old Testament legends about the prophets. Whereas the medieval legend aimed to display the merits of a particular virtue, the Old Testament legend directs attention to the divine authority with which the prophet is endowed, and to whom every person not similarly endowed must submit. Yet the term legend is still the best we can do with the language at our disposal to describe these Old Testament stories; for here also, as in the medieval examples, the story is not really concerned with the biographical details of the hero's life, but involves the hearer directly in what happens. The tale is told in order to edify. It is a matter of obedience and of trust in one's God, who reveals himself *indirectly* through the word or the action uttered or performed by the prophet. In the legend God no longer appears in person, as he did in the saga. The situations in which Elijah or Elisha appear have a typical character, just as those of the saint have also. This is the basis on which the story rests, heavily stylised and standardised. The contrast between good and bad is brought out sharply: on the one hand Elijah, strong in his faith in his god, on the other the idolatrous king. The two unbelieving captains are contrasted with the third, who is a believer.[31]

Here, I believe, Koch is guilty of a mistake in judgment. Elijah and Elisha indeed have a typical character, but it is not that of the embodiment of a virtue. It is instead the rather blank character of a prophet. The reader is in no way called upon to 'go and do likewise' with regard to the prophetic activity of Elijah or Elisha. Even Koch points out that the behavior to be imitated is that of the third captain rather than that of Elijah. In the legends of the saints it is the saints' virtues which are to be imitated, and this is not the case here. It is this confusion which may also be responsible for what I feel is a parallel mistake in judgment on Koch's part when he goes on to discuss 'Legends and Biographies of the Prophets'. There in connection with Jeremiah 28 he observes:

> The medieval term legend is now even less suitable than it was for the Elijah legends, but there is no better term available. For the hearer is still encouraged to emulate Jeremiah, and still to respect Jahweh's word, however unpredictable its coming may be.[32]

This will not do. Jeremiah is simply not presented as a model for emulation. His behaviour with regard to the word of Yahweh is not the focus of these narratives. These narratives about Jeremiah's *via dolorosa* are by no means easy to interpret, especially since the narrator seems deliberately to withhold any interpretive orientation. But to attempt to reconstruct out of this any role for Jeremiah as the example of respect for God's word is not only to read in too much that is not there, but also to miss the challenging question of the significance of this restraint. Here von Rad's words seem to fit the situation much more adequately:

> Jeremiah's sufferings are described with a grim realism, and the picture is unrelieved by any divine word of comfort or any miracle. The narrator has nothing to say about any guiding hand of God; no ravens feed the prophet in his hunger, no angels stop the lion's mouth. In his abandonment to his enemies Jeremiah is completely powerless—neither by his words nor his sufferings does he make any impression on them. What is particularly sad is the absence of any good or promising issue. This was an unusual thing for an ancient writer to do, for antiquity felt a deep need to see harmony restored before the end. Jeremiah's path disappears in misery, and this without any dramatic accompaniments. It would be completely wrong to assume that the story was intended to glorify Jeremiah and his endurance. To the man who described these events neither the suffering itself nor the manner in which it was borne had any positive value, and least of all heroic value: he sees no halo of any kind round the prophet's head. On the contrary, Jeremiah sometimes appears in situations which even a reader in the ancient world might have regarded as somewhat dubious (Jer 38.14-27).[33]

Admittedly, the label prophet story is potently non-descriptive as the label of a literary type. The adjective is purely content-oriented and thus extremely suspect. However, from an examination of the forms of speech used by the prophets it can be observed that they had no forms which were uniquely their own. Instead they borrowed forms or literary types at home in other situations. For this reason we ought to be especially careful in the classification of narratives about the prophets. In this connection Koch is essentially correct when he observes that the 'biography' of Jeremiah is a new literary type, but one which reflects its ancestry. The individual portions of this 'biography' resemble very much the stories about Elijah and Elisha in their literary type. Koch feels, in my opinion correctly, that the writer of this material, presumably Baruch, has employed an older literary form as the building block for the creation of a new one.[34] However, Koch does not go on to point out in sufficient detail the correspondence which exists between this new literary form of prophet biography and that type of historiography which is encountered in the Succession Document, or the parallel correspondence between the older, simpler prophet stories and the so-called hero sagas. I confess to being unable to come up with any suitable labels to apply to this older, simpler type of prophet story which is occasionally called prophet legend, but the breakdown by Otto Plöger[35] into the two sub-categories of prophet deed story and prophet word story is a helpful step. In spite of some difficulties it seems to me best to abide with the label prophet story and to reject the designation prophet legend as misleading for the reasons I have given.

Neither the analysis nor the proposals made here are offered primarily for their acceptance. Instead, as indicated at the outset, the aim is to stimulate discussion. Rather than to air familiar generalities, I have chosen the 'nervy' and risky method of forcing myself to say in one specific case precisely what seems wrong, why it is so, and what, if I had the power, I should do about it. Word usage in scholarly circles is a peculiar matter; where consistently practiced and accompanied by a clear gain in clarity, healthy changes in usage can come about. Especially since influential reference works are now in preparation, now is the time for cooperative effort in proposing and testing possible reforms of usage.

4

BALAAM: SINNER OR SAINT?*

George W. Coats

Balaam was a sinner. Biblical tradition leaves no doubt about the severity of his violations (cf. Num 31.8-16; Deut 23.5-6; Josh 13.22; 24.9-10; Judg 11.25; Mic 6.5; Neh 13.2; 2 Pet 2.15; Jude 11; Rev 2.14). Indeed, two distinct channels of tradition, deriving perhaps from a single original kernel, depict the scarlet character of Balaam's sin. On the one hand, Balaam bears the guilt for seducing Israel into the debacle at Baal Peor (cf. Num 31.16; Rev 2.14). The juxtaposition between the Balaam story, Num 22–24, and the account of Israel's apostasy at Baal Peor in Num 25 may reflect that wing of the traditions. On the other hand, the tradition describes Balaam as a man who sold his divination skills for profit to Balak the king of Moab (cf. Deut 23.5-6; Josh 24.9-10; Neh 13.2; 2 Pet 2.15; Jude 11). In this facet of the tradition Balak hires Balaam to curse Israel, and Balaam agrees, even though Yahweh shows that the people carry his blessing. The digression in Num 22.21-35, a secondary element in the Balaam story itself,[1] may reflect this stage in the development of the tradition.

The negative traditions about Balaam, however, do not readily parallel the story in Num 22–24. In the story Balaam does not seduce Israel. He does not curse them. He blesses them. The point can, of course, be very easily harmonized with the second pole of the negative tradition. Those texts making some allusion to Balaam's plan to curse Israel explain that Yahweh turned his curse into a blessing. Deut. 23.4-6 and Josh 24.9-10 make the conflict of goals between Balaam and Yahweh quite explicit. In Deut 23.5-6: '... they hired against you Balaam the son of Beor from Pethor of Mesopotamia to curse you. But I was not willing to listen to Balaam; therefore he blessed you.' The exegete cannot ignore these texts in interpreting the Balaam story. Yet, interpretation should seek, not simply a harmony between these texts and the Balaam story, but a comparison that will allow the unique character of each to appear. The Balaam story, I believe, is not simply the narrative counterpart for allusions to Balaam's thwarted efforts to curse Israel. It presents Balaam, not as a sinner whose plan for cursing Israel Yahweh foiled by direct intervention, but to the contrary as a saint who intended from the beginning to do nothing other than obey Yahweh's word. The key for sustaining an argument that the story in Num 22–24 characterizes Balaam as a saint lies in an adequate identification of genre. Gressmann defined the story as a saga, with extensive description of details he felt to be characteristic for the genre.[2] This position subsequent interpreters of the story have followed without extensive additions or changes. Moreover, if such a story does belong to the Balaam tradition, its plot line would not be difficult to imagine. Moving in an arc of tension from an introduction of the crisis to its resolution, the story would have described the magician hurrying off to meet Balak at Balak's invitation, delayed perhaps by divine obstruction visible only to the prophet's ass, then arriving in the honor Balak had prepared only to find his repeated efforts to curse Israel turned miraculously into blessing.[3] Noth describes the plot in this way: 'In this tradition it was the efficacious power of Balaam's curse that had to be faced. The superiority of the God of Israel over the curse of the hostile magician ... was demonstrated by turning the usually infallible and real effect of the spoken curse into its opposite, with the result that it brought a blessing upon the Israelites.'[4] But as Noth recognizes, that plot line is a reconstruction based on the allusions in Deuteronomy and Joshua. The story in Num 22–24 does not follow that line. Indeed, it does not follow a plot line at all.[5]

Marked off from the preceding narration by the itinerary formula in 22.1, the story opens in vv. 2-3 with a pattern of structure common to narratives built around a plot. An exposition introduces the principal protagonist, Balak the king of Moab, and describes his plight.[6] He and his people stand in fear of the Israelite hordes poised on their border. The text significantly emphasizes the plight by a stylistic repetition of the note about Balak's fear.[7] The following verses (vv. 4-6) set the subject of the story. Balak intends to hire Balaam to curse the people and thus make his battle more manageable. The motif in v. 6b may well establish a point of dialectic with the patriarchal promise and open an interchange between the story and its larger Pentateuchal context. But such a contact is secondary, not an intrinsic part of the story (cf. in contrast Num 24.9). Rather, v. 6b highlights an interplay between blessing *and* curse from the lips of Balaam as an intrinsic element in the story's narration. So far so good for a plot. At this point we might expect a good story, a tale according to Gressmann's perspective, or at least a battle report like those in Num 20 and 21.

The plot breaks off, however, in vv. 7-14 with a marked difference in movement. These verses introduce a series of scenes, vignettes out of Balaam's life. And with the exception of the digression in 22.21-35, each vignette repeats a single motif about the hero. There is no development of the crisis posed by the exposition. To be sure, there is movement in narration. The principals in the scenes move from place to place. Verses 7-14 and 15-20 in Num 22 show contact between Balaam and the messengers of Balak in Balaam's territory. Verses 36-40 in the same chapter report the initial direct contact between Balaam and Balak. Then a series of sacrifice scenes in 22.41–23.12, 23.13-26 and 23.27–24.14 shift the locale to the battle-field. And each scene is separated from the other by an explicit shift in sacrificial site. But even with this kind of movement in locale from vignette to vignette, there is no movement in plot. Each scene serves only as an occasion to repeat the single motif of the series.

That single motif surfaces in the first scene with Balaam's first speech, 22.8. Balak's messengers have given Balaam the invitation they carry. Balaam's response, however, affronts expectations for a plot development. He does not negotiate over price. He offers no objection at the prospects of cursing Israel. He does not warn Balak's messengers that he can do nothing other than bless Israel. He announces only a statement of his procedure: 'Lodge here tonight and I will bring back word to you as Yahweh speaks to me'. To discover the name, Yahweh, the name of Israel's own God, on the lips of a foreign diviner is somewhat abrupt. The problem, however, cannot be pinpointed by puzzling over the possibilities a foreign diviner might have had to be introduced to Yahweh. That really makes little difference in the development of the story.[8] The problem lies rather in the credibility of the scene. What chance would an envoy have to secure Balaam's curse against Israel when Balaam calls on the name of Israel's God? If a plot line of a good story does lie behind this story, that plot line loses its force with this speech.

But of more importance, the speech introduces a recurring motif, a device for emphasizing a particular virtue in Balaam's character. He neither accepts nor rejects the invitation on his own initiative because his direction in such matters lies completely with Yahweh. Balaam does only what Yahweh tells him to do. This motif appears again in the story in 22.18, 20, 35, 38; 23.3, 5, 12, 16, 26; 24.13-14. The motif can be easily misunderstood, however. The scenes with Balak's messengers illustrate the problem. In the first messenger scene (v. 12), God refused permission for Balaam to curse Israel with an explicit countermand: 'You shall not curse the people, for they are blessed.' The second scene depicts a return of the messengers more honorable than the first, and a renewal of the invitation. And Balaam returns to God for direction in his response. Thus the problem: Why does Balaam return to God? Why did he not simply refuse? Had the invitation not been rejected? Yet, as the story now stands, the focal point is not God's blessing on Israel for all times, with a crisis centered in whether Balaam will transgress God's command and curse what God has blessed. The focal point is not even God's word. It is rather *Balaam's* total dependence on God's word. If God says bless, than Balaam cannot curse. If God should change his mind and say curse, than Balaam cannot bless. The speech in v. 18 is thus significant. Balaam does not say, 'Even if Balak should pay me well, I would not curse God's people'. (Cf. 23.8 where the motif does focus on blessing, not on Balaam's obedience.) Rather, the emphasis falls on Balaam's devotion to God's word, no matter which direction it takes, no matter the consequences. 'Even if Balak should give me his house full of silver and gold, I would not be able to go beyond the word of Yahweh my God to do less or more.'

In the arrival scene, 22.36-40, a distinct dimension of the motif appears. God puts his word directly into Balaam's mouth (cf. Ezek 3.1-3). As an apology for his initial refusal, Balaam explains: 'The word that God puts into my mouth, that must I speak'. The same motif appears in two of the sacrifice scenes, 22.41–23.12 and 23.13-26. In each case Balaam prepares a sacrifice as if uncommitted to one direction or the other.[9] In each case Balaam leaves Balak beside the sacrifice in order to seek Yahweh. And he announces that if Yahweh appears, he will report the word Yahweh gives him accurately. In each case Yahweh puts a blessing into his mouth. And in each case he explains the blessing, not by saying that it is impossible to curse that which is already blessed. The apology centers instead on obedience to each particular word. 'Must I not take heed to speak what Yahweh puts into my mouth?' 'Did I not tell you, "All that Yahweh says, that I must do?"'

The third sacrifice scene, 23.27–24.14, alters the pattern somewhat. The opening lines, 23.27-30, maintain the standard pattern of the first two scenes. Balak presses the ritual, moves Balaam to a new spot, and hopes for a curse on the third try. Balaam follows suit with instructions to build seven new altars, instruction executed at once by the obedient Balak. But in this case, Balaam does not leave Balak beside his sacrifices to seek out an omen. Rather, he *sees* Yahweh's blessing immediately. And he moves accordingly. This shift in pattern, however, does not mean that Balaam assumes God's blessing on Israel.[10] The blessing in each moment depends on Yahweh. 'When Balaam saw that it was good in Yahweh's eyes to bless Israel, he did not go as at the other times to seek omens.' The point is confirmed with Balaam's apology in 24.12-13. Indeed, this climactic speech binds the scene carefully into the unity of the series by citing Balaam's speech to the messengers from 22.18, only slightly expanded. 'Even if Balak should give me his house full of silver and gold, I would not be able to go beyond the word of Yahweh my God to do good or evil on my own.' And the capstone of the story follows: 'That which Yahweh speaks, I will speak'. Thus the climax parallels the second scene in the story, binding the narration, or at least the series of vignettes, into a significant unit. Moreover, the final speech highlights the key motif as static. It does not change from the beginning to the end.[11] Balaam can speak only what God gives him to speak. Whatever that is, whether blessing or curse, Balaam will report.

Structure in the story thus shows that if a story with a plot lies in the background of the text, its plot line has been totally subordinated to the recurring emphasis on Balaam's devotion to Yahweh's word. The purpose of the story as it now stands is not to spin a tale about a foreign diviner who came to curse Israel, but to depict a foreign diviner as a prophet who spoke Yahweh's word and nothing else, regardless of the consequences. That kind of structure is typical for a *legend*. Ronald M. Hals has clarified the genre, as well as the use of the widely abused term *legend* for the genre, by observing that such pieces of literature function to edify. The narration characterizes a particular virtue in the hero as a virtue desirable by all generations of faithful. Would that all of Yahweh's prophets were so faithful to the word![12] Moreover, the hero appears typically as slightly less than superhuman. He never wavers to the right or the left. Balaam is, in short, perfect in his devotion. He is a saint.[13]

James Wharton recognizes the positive character Balaam carries in the story. But he denies that Balaam could be a saint. 'We must be clear that even the enthusiasm for the supremacy of the prophetic word did not serve to make of the Eastern diviner an Israelite "saint" or even a "prophet of Israel" in the full sense.'[14] But his position reflects a fundamental misunderstanding of the story, produced at least in part by failure to recognize that the story is no longer a tale. Wharton explains: 'So outspoken a man as the "later" Balaam appears to be would hardly have been hired to curse Israel if he were a "convert to Yahwism". Rather in the later form of the saga it is the constraint of the prophetic word, rather than the personality of the diviner which is the center of focus. Therefore, it is entirely fitting that one who has accepted hire to curse God's people should meet death at the hands of Israel...'[15] But in the legend Balaam steadfastly refuses hire explicitly to curse Israel. If he accepts hire, he does so with the explicit commitment to pronounce whatever word Yahweh puts into his mouth. Moreover, the word of Yahweh offers no *constraint* on Balaam's direction at all. There is no intervention in Balaam's movement, as there is quite clearly in the digression centering on the ass who can see better than the seer. Balaam begins and ends with the same devotion to speak only what Yahweh gives him to speak. If a saint is defined as the hero of a legend who demonstrates at least one overriding virtue, then Balaam qualifies.

It is important to emphasize here the difference between the purpose of the story as it now stands and the purpose of other elements in the Balaam tradition. Noth observes: 'From the point of view of the history of the tradition, the theme of coming to bless instead of to curse is certainly the primary one. For the purpose of the narrative from the very beginning was, without doubt, the recording of the blessing of the famous Balaam.'[16] That point may well be correct. But the purpose changed in the development of the story to its final stage as a legend. And Noth missed the change. Thus he ponders the embarrassing absence of Balaam's commitment to pronounce only blessing. 'What then is the point of the lengthy treatment of the initial refusal to come...? In spite of the impression of antiquity..., it must be based on later reflection and have the aim of averting from Balaam—and from Yahweh, too—any possible reproach of having deceived Balak. It all takes place in order to make clear to Balak that his desire for a curse upon Israel will not be fulfilled.'[17] But this conclusion misses the point of the narrative. Balaam never commits himself to blessing for Israel apart from repeated inquiry for God's word. There is no aura of deceit, even as Balaam moves from sacrifice to sacrifice. Neither does Yahweh *force* Balaam to succumb to his greater power. In the digression Yahweh's superior power is not the issue. In other occasions of the tradition God *forces* Balaam against his will to depart from his original goal (Deut 23.5). But evidence for that motif *does not appear* in this story. And we must avoid importing evidence from other texts or reconstructions as definitive for Num 22–24. Rather, each scene in this story takes place in order to make clear that Balaam will not give curse *or* blessing on demand. Whether blessing or curse, his word depends each moment on the word Yahweh puts into his mouth. That distinction, that shift from the theme of blessing to a theme of radical dependence on God's word whatever its character, must demand attention if the history of the Balaam tradition is to be fully heard.

Hermeneutical problems arise in this kind of analysis, obviously. But one in particular demands attention here. OT scholarship has made a truism of its assertions about God's mighty acts in Israel's history. Those traditions reporting God's intervention on Israel's behalf, represented by the recitation of events in Israel's early history, stand as the theological foundation for Israel's faith. Wharton observes that 'the ancient recital of the mighty acts of God (cf. Deut 26.5-9) is enriched and expanded by the inclusion of this confessional event [Balaam], which stands as the capstone of the wandering narratives'.[18] Such an emphasis, I believe, misses the thrust of the Balaam story. The story as it now stands in Num 22–24 does not emphasize God's mighty acts. It emphasizes the virtue of a man, his contribution to Israel's well-being, indeed, the well-being of all nations. Must we not reevaluate the positive contribution of such saints to the ongoing process of human experience with God, leading to a culmination of our salvation in the life, death, and resurrection of the man Jesus of Nazareth?[19]

5

TALE

George W. Coats

Old Testament narratives appear in a variety of dresses: legend, tale, saga, novella, fable, history. And the variety can be overwhelming. How does the audience make sense of all of these types? Is there any sense of continuity, of common purpose in the plethora of categories? Indeed, how does the audience even know that all of these types exist? Some awareness of difference from story to story may lie at the base of perception. But is the difference anything more than an obvious difference in content? If at some point the simple statement of multiple forms finally strikes home for the audience, what difference does it make?

At the risk of oversimplification, I would suggest that narrative genres in the Old Testament fall into three recognizable groups: (1) One group develops its narration under the control of a cause-effect sequence of events. The intention of the genres in this group is fundamentally to report the events in their proper sequence. The focus is on the event without an over-abundance of effort for constructing the sequence in order to meet some further goal. Examples of this type of narrative would include anecdote, report, biography, autobiography, and of course history writing. (2) A second group develops its narration under the control of a concern to describe events. But the pattern of control derives, not from the cause-effect sequence of events, but from a concern to narrate the events in an intrinsically interesting pattern. The focus is still on the event. But in this group, the events are constructed in the pattern of a plot. An example of this type is the novella. (3) A third group shifts the focus of the narration away from event, toward characterization of one or more principal figures. Events might still appear in the narration. But the genre diverts the attention of the audience from the event to the characterization. A prime example of this category is legend.

The genre of tale falls into the second general grouping. A distinct plot controls the structure of the tale. Narration of a set of events is certainly present. But the narration is dominated by the plot, not by a commitment to reporting the sequence. The focus of the narrative is not on reporting events as they happened, although the narration doubtlessly assumes a reporting function. The focus is rather on construction of the sequence so that the narration will attract the attention of the audience and hold it until the storyteller is ready to release it. Claus Westermann describes this general pattern of plot as an arc of tension ranging from an initial moment of complication when the attention of the audience first locks onto the narrative power of the storyteller to a resolution of the tension at the peak of the narrative.[1] The final stages of narration would provide some gradual reduction of tension until the concluding lines round off the plot. The pattern might be diagramed as follows:

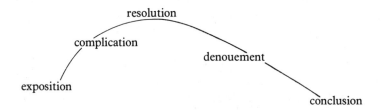

Some explanation of these structural terms is in order. The story opens with some kind of formal exposition, a definition of the principal characters in the narrative and, in some cases, a brief presentation of the situation that holds these characters together in an interesting and significant combination of events. This element of genre provides the information for the audience necessary for the storyteller to narrate his story. The term 'exposition' should not be confused with the same term used in a quite different context to mean a kind of interpretation of some distinct piece, a discursive description of meaning or purpose that might give rise to useful propositions.[2] Its use as a structural term parallels the use of the same term to describe the first part of a musical composition, particuarly when the 'exposition' sets forth principal patterns to be developed in the following parts of the composition. Typically, the exposition begins with some kind of unusual syntactical construction: (1) a sentence with inverted word order (Gen. 21.1); (2) a dependent clause (Gen. 1.1); a nominal construction (Gen. 5.1); or a combination of patterns introduced by *way^{e}hî* (Gen. 6.1).[3]

The second element, the complication, stirs the mixture enough to suggest that the relationships between the principals or the events that embroil the principals are not simple. To the contrary, there is some kind of problem, a crisis in relationships, a threatening turn of events, a hostile confrontation. Indeed, the second element will mix the relationships and events enough so that the audience will experience an increase in tension, mounting to some as yet undertermined breaking point. If the element is effective, it will hold the audience in rapt attention. Indeed, it will intensify the perception of tension for the audience until it simply cannot take them any farther.

The third element in the plot is typically brief and to the point. The tension breaks; to the benefit or the detriment of the hero in the story, the element narrates some kind of resolution for the problem in the plot. It is commonly the case that the resolution of the complication will mark the critical insight into the goals of the story, or at least it will provide some signpost toward that end.

The fourth element, the denouement, stands in tight proximity to the climax or resolution of the plot. It shows the consequences of the critical turning point. It addresses the natural concern of the audience to know what difference the breaking point makes for the principals of the plot. The final element wraps up all loose ends, rounding off the plot with observations that bring the concerns of the audience to a natural conclusion. Olrik observes this characteristic of the genre, described under the German term *Sage*: 'The *Sage* begins by moving from calm to excitement, and after the concluding event, in which a principal character frequently has a catastrophe, the *Sage* ends by moving from excitement to calm'.[4] In outline form, this pattern has the following configuration:

I. Exposition

    A.   General circumstances

    B.   Principal characters

    C.   Events that create 'relationships'

II. Complication

    A.   Problem in relationships

    B.   Events related to the problem that create crisis

III. Resolution

IV. Denouement

    A.   Relaxation of tension in the relationships

    B.   Reconciliation events

V. Conclusion

These observations about structure for the genre built around a plot can apply to both tale and novella. Some distinction between the two genres is now in order. Novella is typically long (a relative qualification), complex in interrelations of structural elements. Indeed, the complexity involves the interrelationship of characters. Sub-plots may appear. Excursuses might interrupt the development of the plot line. Significant asides for characterization may punctuate the interaction of the principals. In contrast, the tale is typically short, although its length may vary from particular example to the next particular example. It is commonly simple in interrelationship of structural elements as well as depiction of relationships among the principal characters. Indeed, the number of characters will rarely exceed three. Olrik observes that the scene will focus commonly on only two of the three, setting those principals in the action in contrast to each other.[5] No sub-plots will appear. To the contrary, the narration will move briskly from the complication to a resolution. The resolution will commonly not involve abstract concepts, ideas that constitute the theology or sociology of the storyteller. To the contrary, the resolution will typically derive from some particular *event*. In contrast to the legend, with its emphasis on the storyteller's characterization of the principal figure in the story, the tale focuses on the event, with a clear assumption that the event has intrinsic value for the audience. To be sure, the event involves the central hero. But it is presented as event, not as characterization of the hero or theological/sociological principle that belongs to the wider context. The intention of the tale would be to narrate the plot for the sake of its entertainment for the audience. The entertainment value might well open the door for apologia. In the entertaining plot, the storyteller can develop moral principles worth passing down to the next generation of witnesses. But those principles would be reflected in the event at the center of the plot and only rarely from external cultural or theological context. 'A narrative that decidedly emphasizes happenings rather than character is a *tale* rather than a story or novel.'[6] The context is, of course, important. It shapes the presentation of the plot. But the intention of the genre derives from the narration of the plot, not from factors imposed on the plot from the outside.

A detailed description of this genre appears in the work of Claus Westermann.[7] The name of the genre showing essentially the characteristics noted above is, for Westermann, *die Erzählung*. That term commonly translates into English as 'narrative'. The connotation of the term is that the story is one that is *told*. The German verb *erzählen* means to tell a story or a series of events, thus, to narrate something. Yet, the English term 'narration' appears to me to carry considerably broader connotations than it would if it were used as a technical term for a particular genre. The term 'tale' clearly refers to a narrative *told* to an audience. I suggest, then, that the term 'narrative' be reserved in English for a reference to a general group of 'narrated' genres, and that the term 'tale' be employed for the particular genre described above.[8]

A few examples will sharpen the definition of the genre. The tale in Exod 15.22-25a reveals precisely the structural pattern outlined above. Verse 22a constitutes the exposition since it sets the scene with two of the principals in the action, Moses and Israel. In addition it places those principals in relationship by describing an event: 'Moses led . . . ' And the location for the event is defined: ' . . . from the Reed Sea . . . into the Wilderness of Shur'. Verse 22b carries the next element of structure, the complication. And, in fact, the complication has crisis proportions: 'They went three days into the wilderness and found no water'. The next element only heightens the crisis: 'When they came to Marah, they could not drink the water of Marah because it was bitter; therefore it was named Marah'. In fact, the heightening underwrites an etiological element in the tale. But the etiology is not secondary for the unity of the plot. Rather, the narration leads through the etiological factor to a resolution of the crisis. And the resolution focuses on the heightened crisis, not simply the initial complication. Moreover, the resolution involves the third principal in the tale. Yahweh provides the means for turning bitter water into sweet. And it is precisely the act of transformation that focuses the plot of the tale. God aids his people in the wilderness. Without his aid, the people would die of thirst. The conclusion of the tale is thus clear; the tale reflects a marked unity. The relationships in the action demonstrate the nature of God's nurture on the one hand, but also the nature of Israel's dependency on the other. Brief, unified, focused on one particular transaction, the tale makes its point and ends.

Exod 17.1-7 carries a similar tale. Again, an exposition names the people of Israel as a principal in the narrative, locates the scene, relates the Israelites to a second principal, Yahweh, and names an event that involves the principals: 'There was no water for the people to drink'. In contrast to Exodus 15, however, the crisis in the tale is not the absence of water. That note is part of the exposition. The complication now follows in vv. 2-3. In this case, the crisis lies in the response of the people to the problem of water. But the crisis is not simply the problem of water. The crisis is the rebellion of the people against Moses and Yahweh. The resolution nonetheless picks up the production of water for the people to drink, suggesting some problem in the history of the tradition, if not in the unity of the plot structure. Where does the rebellion element fit? And how does that problem effect the structure of the unit? Nonetheless, the water problem is resolved and the plot comes to an end. The etiological element in v. 7 does not seem to be as well integrated in the structure of the pericope as it was in Exodus 15. Nevertheless, the same characteristic structure marks the pericope as tale. Indeed, the primary intention of the unit appears, not in the etiological element, but in the depiction of the *event* that resolves the crisis. God grants the petition of Moses for the people. His instructions for Moses' action carry the means for meeting the crisis. And when Moses carries the instructions out, the crisis is resolved. The event is the center of the tale.[9]

The parallel for this tale is in Num 20.2-13. The tradition, again a story about crisis over water at Meribah, follows essentially the same pattern as the Exodus parallel. The people come to a location, now defined as Kadesh, find no water, and then present a suit to Moses for water. The etiology has its ground in the verb for the suit and justifies the name for the locale. But the essential element remains the quest for water. The heroes of the tradition, now Moses and Aaron together, present their request to God and receive instructions for resolving the crisis. The *event* still marks the resolution of the story. In this parallel, however, a new element appears. Moses and Aaron did not carry out the event properly and, as a consequence, lose the right to enter the land. The tradition about their sin is peculiar to the priestly version of the story, a more abstracted element than can be found in the simpler Yahwistic version in Exodus 17. Yet, the story does not lose its generic character. The sin of Moses does not constitute the subject of an abstracted discourse. It is rooted in the *event*. Moses and Aaron did not act as God instructed them. Rather, they acted in a contrary way. They disobeyed God. The point of the element rests on description of an *act*, not some external point or subtle, abstract argument. The unit is thus clearly a tale.[10]

It should be noted here that the story about the spring in Meribah is considerably longer in P than in J. Yet, despite the growth in length, the structure remains simple. Definition of the genre in terms of length is thus a relative qualification. Exod 15.22-27 is short, and the structure moves in a straight line. Brevity can clearly function as a characteristic feature in the structure of this tale. In Num 20.2-13, the storyteller is more expansive. But the structure is still simple. Even with the etiological element as a distraction, the pericope moves without complexity to its conclusion. In the Flood pericope, Gen 6–9, the simplicity in structure is not so obvious. In its present form, the structure of the unit doubles back on itself at various points. Should the genre of the present form be identified, therefore, as something quite different from tale? The problem is made more complex by the source analysis of the pericope. Gen 6–9 is clearly a composite of Yahwist and priestly versions of the same story. When each is analyzed for itself, the structure of the flood story, though still more complicated than the spring tale in Exod 15, is nevertheless uncompromised by excursus or other types of complexity. The focus of the narrative is on the event, indeed, the event of salvation from the flood and not simply the destruction caused by the flood. The point applies to both J and P. Perhaps the redaction that combines the two creates a new genre. One might legitimately explore whether some middle stage between tale and novella emerges here. But at least the genre of the J and the P stories can, despite their greater length, be identified, because of their simplicity, as tale.[11]

In contrast, the story in Gen 24 reveals not only greater length than the tales in the exodus narration, but also greater complexity in development of structure. The narrtor uses excursus, sub-plot, even flash-back to build a complicated account of the servant's quest for a wife for Isaac. Similarity in structure with the tales explored above can still be seen. But the complexity points beyond tale to the more self-consciously constructed novella.[12]

The tale belongs to the repetoire of the storyteller. The setting common for traditions in the class is the oral performance of the story to a particular audience, for the sake of the audience's entertainment, and indeed, for the sake of moral construction. The tale might have been told for itself, a quick act to remember a particular event of the past. Or it might have been simply an episode in a longer performance, one among several tales, legends, fables, songs, or other items that could have composed the oral performance of a saga. In contrast, the novella reflects a more reflective and self-conscious construction. Its character assumes a written setting. And its complexity attests to its artistic patterns in complicated and subtle forms.

The intention of the genre, certainly complex, resisting simple summary in brief assertions, changing from specific case to specific case, can nonetheless emerge with some clarity. Tales function to entertain the audience of the storyteller. And the success of the genre in meeting that goal depends on the artistry of the storyteller. That fact means than the artist has flexibility to construct the tale according to the artist's unique sense of esthetics and ethics. Moreover, that process of entertainment will describe the principals in the plot involved in some kind of *act*. The subject of the tale is event, not characterization. But typically the artist who produces tales preserved in the Old Testament expands the general goals in order to create a sense of identity for the audience. The hero of the tale is not simply a type that might belong to all human beings. The hero belongs to the audience as ancestor, as progenitor of a way of life that defines the religious and social mores of the audience. In an essential way, then, the tale builds identity as well as context for its audience.

6

A THREAT TO THE HOST

George W. Coats

The primary purpose for this essay is to demonstrate the value of genre definition in analysis of a particular pericope. Three parallel texts, Gen 12.10-20, 20.1-18, and 26.1-16, constitute the subjects of the demonstration. These texts are obviously related in some manner. They share a common content, a story depicting a husband who asks his wife to introduce herself as his sister when they come to a foreign land. The purpose for the ruse is self-protection: it would prevent his falling victim to a lecherous host who might dispose of him in order to add her to his harem. But they also share a common structure and genre for communicating the content. An exposition presents principals and describes the problem faced by those figures. The complication derives from the husband's plan to meet the crisis, with a notation of results from the execution of the plan. A peak in the tension of the plot, caused by the position of the woman in a foreign harem, leads to a denouement. The host discovers in some way that he has been deceived. And the woman is restored to her proper husband, along with appropriate gifts. The host's household is healed of whatever threat that might have come with the woman, and the visitors leave the country.[1]

Some problem emerges when one asks about the relationship among these three texts. Traditional criticism of the Pentateuch would begin by defining the sources responsible for each of the three texts. According to standard source analysis, 12.10-20 would derive from J. The parallel involving the same principal characters as protagonists but a different set of antagonists, 20.1-18, would come from the parallel E source. And the third story involving different protagonists from the first two stories but the same antagonist as the second story would come from J.[2] Since the stories are obviously related in some way, one might conclude that one among the three is primary and that the other two depend on that one. Martin Noth argues that the oldest stone in this tell of tales is the Isaac story, 26.1-16. 'This story, as distinct from the two variants in the corresponding Abraham story (Gen 12.10-20 [J]; 20.1b-18 [E]), appears here in a still completely "profane" form . . . It may be that here we find ourselves relatively close to the original form of this frequently utilized narrative material, though we must notice that in Gen. 26 this form is apparently present in a condensed literary formulation, at least at the opening.'[3]

John van Seters defines the problems with pointed insight. (1) The traditional definition of relationship between J and E will not serve the analysis of these three stories. The second Abraham story is, according to van Seters, dependent on the first.[4] Moreover, the Isaac story is also dependent on the Abraham material, a revision of both Abraham stories. That would mean that not only a common literary redaction, if not a single source with its successive revisions, is at hand, but, more to the point, the Isaac story cannot stand as the element that accounts for the origin of the tradition.

The most pressing problem for exegesis emerges, however, when one asks about the intention of each pericope and, indeed, the intention of the tradition about a patriarch who pawns his wife off in an act of deception. There has been no extensive debate about the genre definition of the three stories. Essays in English most commonly refer to these stories as tale.[5] Although some reference to the trilogy as saga does appear, the use of the term seems to be a wooden application of 'saga' as a translation of the German 'Sage'.[6] At this stage in the discussion, I assume that the issue does not focus on the proper genre definition.[7] I assume that the issue concerns what difference (if any) it makes for the exegesis of the stories when the exegete puts all three into the category of 'tale'.[8]

The issue can be focused by some review of previous answers given to the question of intention. Specifically, the issue centers on the function of these three tales as elements in the larger Abraham or Isaac sagas. In what manner does the specific content of the tales contribute to the content of the saga? If the Abraham saga is dominated by the theme of the promise to Abraham for great posterity, does the governing theme of the tales support that larger controlling theme? The title given to the three tales by contemporary scholarship, 'A Threat to the Ancestress', would in fact assume a positive answer to the question, since it suggests that the wife of the patriarch confined to the harem of the foreign host cannot become the ancestress of a great posterity.[9] Von Rad's remark is typical: 'One must remember that the jeopardizing of the ancestress called into question everything that Yahweh had promised to do for Abraham ... What concerns us most is the betrayal of the ancestress, and one must not exactly restrain one's thoughts if they recognize in the bearer of promise himself the greatest enemy of the promise'.[10] But that is not the question before us now. It is rather: What is the intent of the tales themselves? Is the promise theme really at the heart of these tales? Or is the narrative produced by some other concern, the promise element perhaps being imposed from the context as an external, even peripheral factor in the narrative? The issue is fundamentally a problem of methodoogy. What is the intention of each pericope in the trilogy?[11]

I

The first pericope, 12.10-20, is framed by itinerary formulas in 12.9 and 13.1. The exposition in 12.10 marks the occasion for Abraham's travel from his homeland to Egypt as a famine. No narrative element builds on the famine here, as in contrast Gen 42 does. The text uses the famine as an occasion to bring the brothers of Joseph to Egypt, a major narrative element in the Joseph Story. The motif here does nothing more than provide the reason for Abraham to leave his home and the implied protection of his own territory. The famine is not the crisis of the story, the element that carries narrative weight for the story. It is only the occasion. In contrast, vv. 11-16 contain the crisis, the substance of plot for the story. Verses 11-13 set the crisis with Abraham's address to his wife. The apparent crisis is a threat anticipated by the patriarch. Since his wife is beautiful, the lecherous Egyptians will kill him in order to possess her. In order to prevent that tragedy, the patriarch lays a plan of deception: 'Say you are my sister, that it may go well with me because of you, and that my life may be spared on your account'. To argue that she may have in fact been his sister does not affect the exegesis of this text one way or the other.[12] Even if she had been his full sister and that could be proven as an historical fact, it would not alter the development of plot in the story. The question is not some doubt about whether the introduction to the Pharaoh was genuine or fabricated. To the contrary, the story recognizes the assertion as a plot to deceive the Egyptians. It hides the fact that she is in fact his wife. That act clearly puts her status as wife under threat from the acquisitive Egyptians. And the purpose of the plan is explicitly to protect the life of the patriarch.

Verses 14-16 narrate the execution of the plan. The Egyptians responded to Sarah just as the patriarch had predicted. They reported to the Pharaoh that her beauty was praiseworthy. And the woman was taken into the Pharoah's house, with an appropriate payment to Abraham for the privilege. It is important to note that here no reference to a promise for posterity appears anywhere in the scope of the story. The woman's presence in the house of the Pharaoh never receives attention as a threat to the promise, a threat to her position as ancestress of the people. To the contrary, the deception places a threat on the Pharaoh. 'The Lord afflicted Pharaoh and his house with great plagues because of Sarai, Abram's wife.' But the point of the threat is not simply the Pharaoh's act. It is explicitly the presence of Sarah, Abraham's wife, in the house of the Pharaoh. The Pharaoh's act disrupted the patriarch's family. And in concert with the warning in 12.3 against hostile relationships with the patriarch, the Pharaoh feels the brunt of the Lord's curse. It does not matter that the Pharaoh was unaware of his violation. The violation occurred even though the Pharaoh did not know that it was a violation. And as a consequence, the Pharaoh and his house suffered the signs of God's curse. It was Abraham's act of selfish self-protection. And that self-protection produced separation in the family, just as open strife between Abraham and Lot had done.[13] But the Pharaoh suffered the consequence.

Moreover, God's intervention (v. 17) emphasizes the problem of strife and separation in Abraham's family. The plagues attack the Pharaoh because of the woman. And then the Pharaoh responds by restoring the woman to her husband. There is some scolding for Abraham. Verses 18b-19 can be understood as a formal accusation against Abraham for his misdeed. The Pharaoh restores the woman. But he also orders Abraham to leave the country. He is deported. And the storyteller at least implies that he left with the goods given him by the Pharaoh. Abraham profits from the deception.

The story does not address the theme of posterity in any way. There is no element that identifies Sarah as the ancestress of the Israelites, suggesting her role as the mother of many people. To the contrary, the story is about deception, selfish self-protection, separation, plagues on the one who caused disruption in Abraham's family, and an appropriate remedy for the problem. But the issue is larger than an observation about a theme within the limits of the pericope. In what manner does the *context* support identification of 'progeny' as a critical interpretive frame? Polzin draws this point from the reference to progeny in 12.1-3.[14] That element lists two principal promises: 'I will make of you a great nation, and I will bless you'. These promises receive support from a further promise: 'I will bless those who bless you, and him who curses you, I will curse'. A final statement summarizes the weight of the promise, expanding its content into a definition of purpose for Abraham and his family: 'By you all the families of the earth shall bless themselves'. The weight of this pericope obviously falls, not on the promise for progeny, if indeed, the promise to make Abraham a great nation refers to progeny,[15] but on blessing and, by contrast, curse.[16] From the perspective of 12.1-3, the exegete must identify the neighborhood for the tale as one concerned with blessing and curse, not progeny. And indeed, the tale fits well in that neighborhood. The Pharaoh receives a curse in the form of plagues. To abuse the patriarch and his family, even if the patriarch himself might be equally culpable in the abuse, is to invite plagues, separation, loss of intimacy, i.e. the curse.

The pattern of structure in this pericope follows precisely the pattern typical for tale. A situation leads to a crisis, raising tension for the audience in anticipation of a resolution for the problem. The crisis is not an abstract idea, such as: How will the promise to Abraham succeed if Abraham dies from famine or the acquisitiveness of the Egyptians? How will the promise to Sarah succeed if she continues permanently in the Pharaoh's house? To the contrary, the crisis *and* its resolution appear in the narrative dress of an event. An *act* of deception leads to disruption of Abraham's house. An *act* of intervention leads to restoration of Abraham's family. The theme that carries the story is not a promise for progeny, not a threat to the ancestress. To the contrary, it is an act of strife that separates Abraham from the Pharaoh and causes plagues on the household of the king. And indeed, it is an act of strife that separates the patriarch from his wife. In both cases, intimacy that should characterize human relationships vanishes, the fruit of the curse. And not even the Pharaoh's gifts can restore it. Abraham leaves Egypt and its Pharaoh. And separation from the source of blessing is the result for the Pharaoh.[17]

The value of the genre question now appears with clarity. The genre of tale does not work with abstract ideas, propositions about overarching themes, static data that need forceful advertisement. To the contrary, it typically describes events. The point of this story lies in the description of events: separation, plagues, restoration, expulsion. It does not lie in a static theme, unaddressed by any explicit part of the story. There is nothing in the story that would necessarily tie the story to an overarching program built on God's promise to Abraham for a son and then for great posterity. To the contrary, it is a story designed to entertain an audience by showing how the family was broken in the face of a foreign crisis but finally restored by divine intervention.[18] Despite strife between Abraham and the Pharaoh, strife that breaks Abraham's family, God restores the broken family and at least offers a chance to restore the broken intimacy.

II

The second pericope, 20.1-18, is similar in structure to the parallel in ch. 12. Yet, remarkable differences mark the second Abraham story as a distinct element in the tradition. The story begins with an itinerary formula that connects the pericope with the context, identifying the place for the events that follow. But there is no clear exposition for the unit. Rather, the narration moves immediately to the complication. In v. 2a, Abraham tells (his hosts?) that Sarah is his sister. There is no reference to fear, no allusion to the beauty of the woman. He simply announces that Sarah is his sister. Moreover, the consequences of the announcement, the complication in the story, appear quickly and in compact form. In v. 2b, the storyteller reports that the king of Gerar took Sarah into his harem. In this pericope, resolution dominates the pattern of the story. Verses 3-16 report the divine response to the crisis and the king's execution of the instructions given him by God. In the exchange between God and the king, God threatens the king with death. The story might thus again be entitled, 'Threat to Abraham's Host', rather than 'Threat to the Ancestress'. The king responds with a profession of innocence, and God accepts the statement. But in addition to the acquittal, God specifies what the king must do to survive the threat. The instructions are carried out, again with an accusation against Abraham for setting up the threat. Abraham defends himself, on this occasion with an allusion to the people in his host country as failing in fear of God and to Sarah as a woman who was indeed his half-sister. But it should be noted that neither reference excuses Abraham's role in the breaking relationships. Abraham's introduction of the woman as his sister caused the disruption in relationships. Indeed, v. 13 suggests that Abraham had developed quite a business with his game. And only God's intervention diverted his unfaithful business from its path toward total tragedy, permanent loss of intimacy.

The final element in the structure comes in vv. 14-16. Abraham receives his wife again. But he also receives the fees for the occasion from the king. In exchange for the transaction, Abraham intercedes for the king, and the king's house is restored. Blessing replaces the curse. And Abraham's own house finds its proper pattern of intimacy restored.

It is important to note that even though transformations have altered the shape and content of this story in comparison to the parallel in ch. 12, the story remains a *tale*. It focuses on a plot that develops around particular events. Indeed, the critical events for the plot duplicate the events in the structure of the tale in ch. 12. Deception leads the king to take Abraham's wife into his own harem. This separation of the blessed family, with adultery only potential, produces a potential execution for the king. The tale focuses on the event that demonstrates what happens to anyone who disrupts the blessed family, even though the guilty party was not aware of his role in the disruption and not guilty of the actual crime of adultery.[19] At no point in the development of the story is the issue Abraham's progeny or God's promise for progeny. To the contrary, the tale itself depicts events that describe relationship to the source of divine blessing. And that relationship is negative.

Polzin observes, however, that the neighborhood builds on the theme of progeny. Chapter 21 reports the event of Isaac's birth.[20] Yet, some caution must rule here. At no point in the story itself is progeny or Abraham and Sarah the issue. That theme is the opening moment in ch. 21. But neither the threat story in ch. 20 nor the birth story in ch. 21 establishes an explicit connection that would carry the concern for a child in the birth tale back to the tale of a threat to Abraham's host. Indeed, the tale about the birth of Isaac loses its focus on birth, progeny, and the implied connection with the promise. The arc of tension that carries that tale is the strife between Isaac and Ishmael, a duplication of the strife between Sarah and Hagar.[21] To be sure, the tale reports the birth of Isaac. But the narrative develops, not on the theme of promise fulfilled, but rather on the theme of strife and rejection. Even the note in 21.6 about laughter reflects the theme of strife: 'God has made laughter out of me; every one who hears will laugh at me'. If the neighborhood gives the tale in ch. 20 character, it is the character of a tale about strife and curse. And that character corresponds to the structured content of the tale about deception and separation.

III

The third piece in the trilogy, 26.1-17, again alters the structure of the pattern with an obvious element. Between the exposition in v. 1, noting that Isaac went to Gerar because of a famine, with an explicit comment about similarity with the Abraham story, and the complication for the story developed from the wife-sister theme in v. 7 comes a long speech from God set in a theophany. The speech instructs Isaac, who faces famine and thus the traditional trip to Egypt in order to buy food, not to go to Egypt but to stay in Gerar. Then attached to the intervention element is a renewal of the promise to Abraham, Isaac's father, for posterity and land, with the corresponding blessing for all the nations of the earth through the progeny of Isaac.[22] The complication comes in v. 7, with the patriarch's deceptive introduction of his wife as his sister.

But no disruption of the patriarch's family occurs. The king of Gerar does not take her into his harem. And no plague attacks the people of the host country. Rather, the woman remains with her husband/brother. The king discovers the deception when he observes Isaac playing with the woman and concludes that she must be his wife. The typical elements emerge for this story with the king's accusation against Isaac and Isaac's lame excuse. But here the tradition is again transformed. There is no separation between patriarch and wife, an event that would bring curse on the hosts. But the *threat* of curse was there. Someone in the host country might have 'taken' the woman, thinking that she was available. And that act would have brought curse on the hosts. But the result of Isaac's deception was averted. Nothing happened. And when the king discovered the deception, he issued a royal decree protecting the woman and her husband. There is no separation here, no strife with the host. The danger is only potential. Moreover, the discovery of the deception is not the result of divine intervention, protecting both host and patriarch from disaster, but the result of chance that opened the eyes of the host to the identity of the woman. The discovery might be rooted in divine protection. But the point is at best only implicit. The character of the pericope as tale is doubtlessly apparent. But it is no an obvious conclusion as it was for the other two parallels. An event is still central. But its character as the subject for a narration is not as dramatic as in the parallels. The king discovers the deception before the event of strife occurs. And the structure concludes with the patriarch invited to remain in the land. Verses 12-13 note that Isaac did that and became very rich, not from the night's labor of his wife/sister but from the good fortune of his farming. Moreover, the promise element disrupts the structure of the exposition, adding to the amorphous character of the unit. It is significant that only here does the promise, not just for progeny but also for the land, play any role in the tradition. That factor also explodes the simplicity of the story as tale.

What conclusions might be drawn from these factors in the description of genre for the unit? A typical evaluation of the relationship binding the three tales together suggests that the Isaac story is primary and the two Abraham tales develop from the original.[23] This particular suggestion about tradition history reflects the larger hypothesis that the primary factor in the patriarchal theme is the tradition about Isaac. The Abraham tradition and the Jacob tradition would in some manner derive from the original formulation of tradition around the figure of Isaac. Indeed, the more fragmentary character of the Isaac tradition, the simpler and briefer form of the tale, would argue for this position.[24] More recently, however, doubts about this hypothesis have been raised. John van Seters suggests that the primary tale of the trilogy is 12.10-20, the Isaac story being cast as a revision of its Abraham counterpart.[25] I would suggest that the present strictly form-critical, genre-critical examination of the three tales supports van Seters's argument. The Abraham tales reveal a structure that is simple, facilitating the goals of the genre. And neither has any sign of influence upon the structure of the unit from the promise for progeny. The Isaac story is more diffuse in structure, still a tale but not serving the function of tale so clearly. The genre is breaking down here, showing signs of development into something new. And significantly, it is in this pericope that the promise theme appears in explicit form. Even here, the promise appears to be secondary, inserted at the beginning of the story without care for integration with the overall story.[26] Thus, questions about genre facilitate not only the exegesis of the pericope, but also the larger, more technical task of tradition history. One might imagine a tale with the promise reported as a primary event at the center of the plot. The argument of this chapter does not suggest that the genre 'tale' cannot contain the promise theme as a primary item of content. It suggests, rather, that in these three particular tales, promise for progeny is not a factor in the essential content and the structure that carries it. Indeed, the one tale that does contain a promise element shows evidence that the typical characteristics of the genre are breaking up.

If the three tales do not belong to a larger theme controlled by the promise for progeny, with marked transformations around that theme from one stage to another, what kind of larger theme do they belong to? Most recently, Polzin has defined 12.1-3 as the sign for the thematic unity of the larger context for these tales. I agree with this definition of structure, established by the unit in 12.1-3. But I do not agree that the character of the theme defined by 12.1-3 is controlled by a promise for progeny and land. To the contrary, the focus is on blessing.[27] In the larger pattern, especially for the Yahwist, the blessing theme stands in contrast to a narrative motif controlled by the curse, exposed in terms of strife, separation, and the corresponding 'plagues' that affect those who separate themselves from the source of God's blessing. These three tales fit perfectly into the neighborhood.

The principal goal for this essay was to demonstrate the value of genre analysis for exegesis. The hypothesis for analysis defines each of the three stories under consideration as *tale*. Since tale functions as a form of story that builds on a plot structure in order to present an event in a manner that is intrinsically interesting, that proffers entertainment for the audience by shaping the description of the event to build suspense, the genre offers effective communication for the tradition about deceiving a host. Moreover, in each of the three examples, the focus of the genre on event in a plot structure shows the intention of the example to be rooted in some manner in the event, not in a superstructure behind the event. In all three cases, the event of deception perpetrated by the patriarch leads to appropriation by the host of the wife introduced as sister, or at least to the potential for such an event. The deception disrupts the family relationships for the patriarch as well as the relationship between the patriarch and the host. But the intention of the tale does not lie in description of the disruption event. To the contrary, God or chance functions to turn the broken relationship back to some degree of reconciliation. Again, the focus of the genre on event, not theological proposition, shows the intention of the story to be a description of circumstances that obtain for people who support the patriarch in contrast to circumstances that obtain for people who deny support for the patriarch. Even in the face of the patriarch's involvement in causing the strife, strife with the patriarch leads to curse. And the genre of 'tale' functions effectively, not to make that point as an abstract and static proposition, but to depict the events that show the reality of that strife with dramatic clarity.

7

NOVELLA

W. Lee Humphreys

'But it's the truth even if it didn't happen.'
Chief Bromden in Ken Kesey's *One Flew Over the Cuckoo's Nest*

Of the several genre designations employed in the exegetical study of the Old Testament, novella perhaps betrays most clearly its origins in later western literary history and analysis. It is a borrowed term, for novella primarily denotes a narrative type that has developed in the west since the fourteenth century. Yet the term is being used in Old Testament study, and it is our goal in this essay to demonstrate its usefulness.[1] First, however, we must consider the genre novella as defined in recent literary analysis.

1. *Novella in Recent Literary Study*

Clearly the word 'novella' is linked to the word 'novel'. In fact, the latter is an English transliteration of the Italian *novella*. The links between the novella and the novel are two-fold. On the one hand, the novel historically developed from the novellas that took classical shape in the period from the fourteenth century, with the example of Boccaccio's *The Decameron* (c. 1348) generally cited as the best known and most typical. These short prose narratives provided both rudiments of form as well as themes, typical characters, and plot outlines for later novels. On the other hand, novella is currently used in literary criticism to denote a type of prose narrative that stands between the novel and the short story, sharing characteristics of each. Henry James, for example, used the French term *nouvelle* in this latter sense, and others have coined such terms as 'novelette' or 'short novel'.

Because novella denotes a literary form standing intermediate between novel and short story it is best to begin with a brief consideration of what the latter have in common and in what ways they are distinct.[2] First, points held in common:

1. Both short stories and novels are fiction. They do not report events or describe persons as they actually took place or lived in the past. However true to life they must be—and we shall see that they must be true to life in a fundamental sense—they are not historical. This does not, of course, preclude the appearance in them of personages and events from the area of history; what is reported in them is not designed, however, to meet any tests of historical accuracy.

2. Novels and short stories are narratives built around a plot that moves from the establishment of a tension through complications to its resolution. The plot will comprise one or more stress situations or events. They are more than descriptions of places or persons, and they are distinct from reflections of an essayist about a topic or situation.

3. They are prose, not poetry, although poetic units of a variety of types may be utilized in them, as indeed may a wide range of other literary forms (letters, reports, visions).

4. Both are the conscious creative work of generally a single author. They are not folk products that evolve over time. Both may use motifs, themes, plot structures, and characters drawn from the realm of folklore and popular oral and written traditions. Nevertheless, they reveal from beginning to end the artful stamp of a single careful controlling craftsman. They are furthermore designed to be read rather than heard. While having limited links perhaps with oral forms, novels and short stories are artistic written compositions and not simple recorded recitations or outlines for the same. They represent a clear artistic break with oral tradition and are rooted in a life setting characterized by a high level of literacy.

5. Novels and short stories are literary works submitted to the twin tests of aesthetic success and imitative accuracy or truth. They intend to entertain, and this is accomplished in part, at least, by holding out to the reader an aspect of life as it really is. Unlike the historical record or narrative, they depict not so much what happened as what happens in life. Even when set in the distant past or exotic contexts, it is our world and our humanity that we meet as we read them. It is the truth we find, even if it did not happen.

All this the novel and short story have in common, and the novella, standing between them in length, can be so characterized as well: it is an artfully crafted piece of prose fiction that entertains and seeks to give an accurate depiction of life.

There are differences between short stories and novels as well, and consideration of these will help define the unique place of the novella:

1. Most obvious, of course, is length. Short stories are just that: short, easily read in one brief sitting. Novels can range over many hundreds of pages.

2. The number of characters and events encompassed in a short story is limited. One character, or at most a very few, is depicted and usually in one or a limited chain of events or situations. Generally the time frame for the short story is brief. Novels may have so many important characters that the reader needs a chart to guide them through. And a complex and extended chain of events or situations characterizes the novel; in fact, there may well be more than one such chain with varied degrees of inter-relatedness. The time frame can range from a few hours to centuries.

3. In some ways the most essential distinction is that the short story *reveals* the nature of a character or a situation while a novel *develops* characters or situations. James Joyce speaks of the 'epiphany quality' of the short story, its quality of revelation. Through a compact series of events or stress situations a character is made clear and distinct to the reader or a situation's true quality is revealed. By contrast, over a much wider range of events and situations the characters of a novel grow and/or deteriorate; they are seen to evolve as they shape and are shaped by events and situations.

At this point the novella can be brought into sharper focus as falling between the two types discussed. Of course, boundary lines that are too sharp between short story, novella, and novel must not be drawn, for they shade into each other. But genuine differences are apparent. The novella shares all the novel and short story have in common. Longer than the short story, it nevertheless also has a compactness with regard to both the number of characters and the range of events. Generally but one chain of events is followed and usually over a limited time frame. Yet like the novel its primary emphasis is on the development of—and not simply the revelation of—characters and/or situations. Within a compressed frame of time and limited events, characters evolve. Along with the oft-cited *Billy*

Budd by Herman Melville, *The Turn of the Screw* by Henry James, and *Heart of Darkness* by Joseph Conrad, we can suggest that John Steinbeck's *The Pearl* depicts the essence of the novella in recent literature.

2. *Novella and Old Testament Literature*

As we turn to the Old Testament we must acknowledge, at least, the question as to the suitability of a genre term so rooted in later western literary history and criticism for analysis of ancient Hebraic material standing worlds apart from the primary context for the novella. There is no comparable term in Hebrew for a type of literature akin to the western novella. But then, with quite limited exceptions, there is little in the way of genre terminology in the Hebrew Bible, and most of the designations used in form critical analysis come from other areas and periods. The essential issue is not the presence or absence of genre terms in the Hebraic tradition, but of material that essentially fits the descriptive criteria that define a specific genre designation.

Clearly there are no novels in the Hebrew Bible. The extended works contained therein are either collections of materials of varied types or have a style and intent not in line with the novel, e.g. the extended historical corpora of the Deuteronomistic circle or the Chronicler. On the other hand, there do appear to be short stories. Genesis 24 and Ruth would fit this category, and the stories of Daniel 1–6 and Jonah might be noted as well (Jonah with its great fish and rapidly growing plant has elements characteristic of fables, and this element of the miraculous is even more pronounced in Daniel 1–6). Each is brief and reveals the quality of a situation and/or character. Jonah, Ruth, and even Daniel and his companions are essentially the same at the end of each story as at the outset; they do not grow or develop before us. We just recognize with greater clarity the character of each as the story progresses. They share in the 'epiphany quality' of which Joyce spoke.

There also seems to be a limited range of novellas or novella-like material in the Hebrew Bible as well. The story of Samson in Judges 13–16, Joseph and His Brothers in Genesis 37–50, and the story of Esther and Mordecai in the Book of Esther are primary examples, and one must take note of Judith and Tobit in the Jewish and Protestant Apocrypha as well (although elements of the fable appear in the latter). These units are longer than the short stories, and they depict the clear development of central characters or situations rather than simply reveal them. We might further suggest that units like the succession narrative of 2 Samuel 7–20 and 1 Kings 1–2 and the story of Saul in 1 Samuel 9–31 reveal characteristics of the novella and might therefore be designated 'historical novellas'. While offering what is claimed to be an account of public events that altered the course of Israel's history and dealing with significant historical figures, the latter are depicted as evolving through time and are reflective not just of what happened but of what happens to human beings. They attempt to meet the standards of historical truth for their day, but they betray novella-like characteristics as well.

At this point we are in position to offer a description of the genre novella as revealed in the Hebrew Bible, accenting characteristics noted above as constituent of it. Illustrative examples in this essay will be drawn from the Joseph narrative in Genesis. In the following essay this description of the novella will inform an analysis of the Book of Esther.

3. *The Old Testament Novella*

a. *The Novella as Fiction*

The Novella has been defined as the creative product of an artist's imagination. It is not an account of events and persons that bears the stamp of historical reporting and interpretation. As we noted above and will discuss further below, the novella gives an account, not simply of what happened, but of what happens. One comes to it expecting not information about what once occurred on the stage of history, but entertainment and insight into what happens to men and women in life.[3]

This does not mean that there may not be links between the novella and the historical narrative. The novella, like the historical report, is generally set in the past, in a particular time and place, and may well take the form of an account of a series of events as if they had occurred. But it is the essence of the novella that it is not confined to public events available for the world to witness and assess. The novella moves easily into the private and personal, reporting intimate conversations and often even the thoughts of the characters in a detail that would be available to no one but their

creator. Thus in the Joseph narrative we find not only events of a
public nature recalled, such as Joseph's successful audience before
Pharaoh and his promotion to high office (Gen 41), but also private
thoughts of the brothers as they plot Joseph's destruction (37.18-20),
unsuccessfully seek his release (37.21-22, 26-27), later realize their
guilt (42.21-22), and fear revenge on his part (50.15).

The major characters of a novella may be historical figures, and
events from history may be incorporated into the plot. But it must be
stressed that the intent is not to report historical activity.[4] The
historical figures and events are caught up into an imaginative fabric
produced by the creative activity of an author. Thus, Joseph and the
other sons of Jacob may well be historical personages, and there quite
likely was a descent into Egypt by ancestors of what in time came to
be Israel. But simply to read the Joseph narrative as an account of the
lives of those persons and as a description of events in the prehistory
of Israel, or even as some suggest, as reflections of the history and
interrelationships between the several tribes represented by Jacob's
sons is to miss the potential impact of the story and misuse the
material.[5] Indeed, for all of its specificity, a historical inexactness
pervades the Joseph narrative just at the points of its possible linkage
with the history of Egypt. The Pharaoh or even the ruling dynasty is
not named, nor are events dated relative to known persons or events.
Some familiarity with Egyptian custom and practice is reflected in
the narrative lending it a touch of verisimilitude, but it is impossible
in what is presented to root the story in any of the reasonably well
documented periods of the history of Egypt.

Just as in recent western literary study it is possible to qualify the
term novel with the designation 'historical', so, we have noted, it is
possible to speak of a 'historical novella' in the Old Testament. Again
the lines cannot be sharply drawn between the two. Yet the Joseph
narrative and the succession narrative would seem to be illustrative
of each. In the former there is little that is clearly historical; the latter
seems much more firmly rooted in the public events of Israelite
history. Yet, there is a marked quality of the private and interior that
pervades both works, reflective of the creative imagination of an
author, and the latter seems also designed to entertain and inform
about life as well as report events important in the development of
the state of Israel.

It is indeed possible for later generations to treat a novella as
history, as a report of what happened, and to utilize it as such. Thus

the Joseph narrative, once an independent composition, was in time utilized within the larger narrative framework of the Pentateuch, effecting the transition from the three patriarchs in southern Palestine (Genesis) to the tribes in bondage in Egypt (Exodus).[6]

b. *The Novella as Prose*

The novella is prose rather than poetry. It is a prose that not only describes events but depicts conversations between characters. The extended interchanges between Joseph and Pharaoh in Genesis 41 and between Joseph and his brothers later are examples of a developed narrative art. While the novella is a prose composition, it may contain a number of other literary forms as well. The Joseph narrative has set within it several reports of dreams and their interpretation (Gen 40, 41), a formal court speech (44.18-34), and, perhaps as secondary additions brought into the narrative in its later use in the larger Pentateuch, genealogical lists (46.8-37), blessings (48.15-16, 20), and ancient tribal poetry in the form now of a patriarch's last words (Gen 49).

c. *Setting—Time and Place*

The events of a novella are set in a particular time and place that is defined with enough specificity to locate the action. However, we have also seen that often there is not the specificity of detail that allows the events to be as firmly rooted as we would demand of a historical report. In the Joseph narrative the time for the story is, from the perspective of author and reader, the distant past of the patriarchal ancestors of Israel. The narrative's time frame takes in many years as Joseph is transplanted from Palestine to Egypt and transformed from a youth to a mature man of stature and with a family of his own. Often gaps of several years are traversed without effort (e.g. between chs. 37 and 39). The most specific descriptions of the passage of time are the seven good and then seven lean years and the notice of 'two full years' between chs. 40 and 41. The passage of several years linking the events of chs. 42 and 43 is noted with less precision.

The setting moves from the land of Canaan to Egypt and then back and forth several times as first Joseph and then his brothers and father move from Canaan to Egypt. These movements are accomplished with minimal notice and with ease. As we have noted, the author enters into some detail in presenting the Egyptian setting of the story in an attempt to provide verisimilitude for his work. This ranges from the use of Egyptian loan words and names through the mention of several customs and practices characteristic of what for him and his reader is an exotic if not ominous land. The details of the dreams and of the protocol of the royal court (Gen 40–41) seem generally accurate with regard to the situation in Egypt, even if not specific enough to permit the events to be located in a particular time. In a few instances, however, especially with regard to the author's notice about Egyptian distaste for shepherds and their unwillingness to dine with Hebrews (Genesis 46.34; 43.32), he moves beyond the verifiable and even the plausible in the service of a good story. These notices serve a narrative function—allowing the brothers to be alone with Joseph at a critical moment and permitting their settlement in Goshen—and they contribute to a sense of wonder at the strange land of Egypt. But if pressed, they would make the position of Joseph, who is always known to be of Hebrew origin (40.15), quite impossible.

d. *Plot*

The essential skeletal framework of the novella is provided by the plot. The series of events that comprise the plot is not an accidental collection of happenings but a carefully woven fabric, extended over time and set in a distinct locale. The novella has a beginning in which a problem or tension is set out, a middle in which the tension becomes ever more complicated, and an end in which the tension is resolved and the complications vanish. While separated sometimes by large blocks of time and expanses of space, the events that comprise the plot are carefully integrated, growing out of and leading into each other. They cannot stand alone as distinct and complete stories, as can, for example, the several distinct units that make up the cycles dealing with Abraham and Jacob. Each of the latter has a beginning, middle, and end, and most can stand alone. They are but lossely bound into a cycle. Only in rare instances is information contained in earlier units essential for the development of a later saga.

In the Joseph narrative the several units are more akin to the scenes of a play, interlocked with and evolving into and out of each other. They cannot stand alone. The basic tension is set at the outset as we are introduced to a family rift by hatred and seemingly intent on its own destruction. Older brothers are jealous of their youngest sibling and more than willing to act on their hatred to rid themselves of this thorn in their lives; the youngest is a spoiled brat, telling tales on his own brothers and boasting of dreams that set him over them and their patents; an old and doting father sparks and feeds the flames of jealousy through favoritism shown the much loved youngest son. The brothers do act and apparently rid themselves of their youngest brother, and all that remains is cruelly to deceive their father. Genesis 37 sets the narrative in motion; the tension is defined and the main characters carefully sketched.

Then for a time the story leaves the family in Canaan and follows the adventures of the youngest son as he moves, in the best 'rags to riches' tradition, from Egyptian slavery and the depths of obscurity in a house of detention to a position second only to Pharaoh in power over all the land. By the end of Genesis 41 Joseph has become vizier over Egypt, has married into the family of the priest of the Sun God, is busily implementing his strategy to meet the crisis of famine, and is thoroughly Egyptianized. It would appear at first glance that we have abandoned the tension set out in the beginning (with the intrusive ch. 38 reinforcing this impression) to take up a new story. In fact, some have suggested that we have in Genesis 39–41 (with 47.13-26 and 50.20) an old and distinct story of the remarkable rise of a Hebrew lad into the Egyptian royal establishment, with its own beginning, middle, and end, its own tension, complication, and resolution.[7] No clear links bind Genesis 39–41 with ch. 37, and none are needed. Genesis 37 does, however, explain how the young man came to Egyptian slavery (compare 40.15), and the famine of Genesis 41 is said to afflict the whole earth, bringing many people to Egypt for relief. This once possibly independent story of Joseph's rise and success in Pharaoh's court stands as a kernel at the heart of the larger story of the family of Jacob, into which it is now bound.

Suddenly Joseph's brothers reappear after many years, and the tensions set out in Genesis 37 are recalled and soon complicated. Driven by famine from Canaan to Egypt, the brothers encounter only trouble, as this high official takes such ominous interest in their lives and family situation, makes wild and unfounded charges against them, jails all for a brief period, then Simeon for longer while the others are sent home with provisions, their money secretly returned, and instructions not to appear again without their new youngest brother (who apparently was born in the intervening years, during which Joseph's mother also dies since she is not mentioned after ch. 37). A second trip to Egypt some years later only further complicates the family situation. The second reception seems at first the antithesis of the first, but the brothers' brief respite leads in the end to further accusations and the gravest of dangers to Benjamin, the father's latest favorite. A number of links bind this scene with what has come before. Only as the tension becomes unbearable is resolution attained. Joseph reveals his true identity—which at first can only spark terror—and then makes clear that he, like the brothers, has changed and forgives all. He then uses his position of power in Egypt to resolve a subtension introduced by the famine and the danger it poses for the family of Jacob. All are brought to Egypt and settled in Goshen. In time Jacob dies with all his sons about him, and before Joseph's own death the brothers are again reconciled (50.15-21). A family that once seemed clearly doomed to self-destruction has been preserved.

The plot is complex in its movement through time and over great expanses of space. A subplot dealing with the remarkable rise of Joseph in Egypt stands within, facilitating the transformation of the hero from an abused youth into a powerful official. This subplot is integrated into the larger story through the motif of the famine and the danger it poses for all the earth; the position Joseph attains in Egypt permits both the complication and final resolution of the tension set out at the beginning. Each scene builds on what came before and grows naturally out of it. Each opens upon what follows. The scenes cannot stand alone; prior material is assumed, and expectations are raised that demand resolution in what follows. Even when the family is set aside for a time and we follow Joseph through his adventures in Egypt, the larger tension remains in the background; we know the brothers are not rid of this rival for their father's affections, for while he is seemingly lost to them he is in Egypt, alive and growing in power. Is it possible they will meet again? Earlier tensions linger in the reader's mind and leap back to center stage with the notice of the world-wide famine and the fact that people from all corners of the earth are coming to Egypt for relief (41.54, 57). The subplot is artfully integrated into the larger narrative.

e. *Characterization*

As the plot evolves the characters of a novella develop. It is this development of characters that essentially sets the novel and novella apart from the short story. Human beings grow and disintegrate before our eyes as the plot runs its course. The figures we meet at the outset are not the same at the end, and more than outward circumstance is altered (contrast Ruth). The characters of a novella can range from stereotypes to full-bodied and complex individuals. Thus Joseph the spoiled and boastful brat of Genesis becomes a powerful official, able and skilled in his new position, but still ruthless in his treatment of his brothers and father. Whether or not his treatment of them in Genesis 42–44 is designed as a test, he toys with them over a span of many years, arbitrarily detaining and releasing them, accusing them unjustly. Even his return of their money serves only to terrify. Yet through it all he changes, and this is made clear as he responds to changes in them. At first overcome as he listens in on their self-accusations (42.24; 43.30-31) he later reassures them of his compassion and care. The feared official who so long toyed with their deepest feelings and lives, as a cat with a mouse, allowing even his old father to believe him dead for many years, finally acknowledges that he is not god-like (50.19). Yet that was just the posture he assumed for so many years.

The others change as well. The bitter brothers are humbled and show themselves able in a crisis to take action to save a younger brother when again they might forfeit him and escape from a difficult situation. Chapter 44 nicely parallels ch. 37 in this respect. They are no longer the jealous men of the opening scene, even if to the very end they still entertain some uncertain.y regarding Joseph (50.15-18). Jacob also evolves from a man who loves too much and not wisely, and who is all too prone simply to surrender to seeming tragedy (37.34-35; 42.35-38), to one who can take charge of a situation (43.11-14) and demonstrate a dignified self-restraint as an honored old patriarch who meets even Pharaoh as an equal (47.7-11).

It is around these figures that the story evolves, and they evolve with it. The remaining characters are but props, ranging from the Pharaoh through the Butler and Baker and even Potiphar and his wife to Joseph's steward. They facilitate the action but remain flat and unchanging. The central figures comprising the family of Jacob are multi-faceted, however, and the story is theirs. The reader can feel sympathy with the brothers' outrage at Joseph's tale-bearing and boastful recounting of his dreams; our feelings go out to them, but their actions cannot be condoned. We can also sympathize with an old father's doting on the youngest of his children, the only sons of his beloved wife. We understand his fierce attachment to Benjamin as a replacement for the lost Joseph. But this single-minded attachment to Joseph and Benjamin can only result in rending the fabric of family harmony, and this the reader must recognize as well. In fact, at the outset and perhaps through most of the narrative, Joseph appears the least appealing figure, and the change he undergoes is the most profound. No doubt the author of this novella has drawn from the older folk traditions of Israel this collection of figures and can assume that the reader is essentially acquainted with them and their relationships. But he has shaped them into a set of distinct and complex individuals with the sure hand of a literary master.

f. *The Creative Work of an Author*

Hermann Gunkel, the father of form critical analysis of the Old Testament, described the novella as an expansion of a form called saga.[8] It was largely his study of Genesis that led him to this understanding of the origin of the novella. It was clear to him that if the very brief units dealing with Abraham and Jacob were sagas, the much longer and more complex Joseph narrative could not be so classified. Yet, he believed the latter to be rooted firmly in the former. The Joseph narrative was too multi-faceted in its integrated fabric of episodes and range of characters to qualify as a saga. He rightly defines it as a novella. However, his conclusion that it was thus a development, through multiplication of episodes, addition of long speeches, an increase of characters, of an older saga goes beyond the evidence and seems contrary to the basic characteristics of the novella. Sagas are rooted in the folk levels of a people or tradition and have behind them a long history of oral recitation. They are the product of a community even if their transcription into their present written form is the work of one person. That person stands at the end of a long process of creative adaptation and transmission, and while he/she may engage in some shaping of the material, it seems inappropriate to speak of that person as an author.

We have defined the novella as the literary creation of an individual, an artfully crafted piece from the hands of an author. The complexity of characterization, the extended and integrated series of episodes that comprise the plot of the Joseph narrative are better comprehended as the work of a literary craftsman and the narrative a written composition from the outset, than as the expansion of brief units of the sort that comprise the cycles dealing with Abraham or Jacob. Motifs may be borrowed from folk lore in the composition of a novella; for example, the motif of the vengeful rejected woman of Genesis 39 or that of the younger brother who rises above his older siblings are found in the folk traditions of many peoples.[9] And clearly the characters of the Joseph narrative are dawn in part from the folk traditions of Israel.

g. *Intention*

It is always an imposition to attempt to divine the intention of an author. Yet certain literary forms lend themselves to certain purposes and are designed to attain distinct ends. The author of a novella seeks to entertain. A good story is told and told well. Characters that engage the interest of the reader initiate, pass through, and react to a series of events that may amuse, excite, or frighten the reader. We are caught up in and awed by the prospects of a family that seems about to self-destruct. We marvel at the sudden rise of Joseph in the alien land of Egypt, are intrigued by the first reunion of the brothers when only one side recognizes the other, share the discomfort of the brothers when wrongly accused and jailed by the one they wronged, are amused by the irony of the brothers being believed when they lie (37.30-31) but treated as liars when they speak the truth (42.7-14), are ready to explode, like Joseph, with the tension at the end of the second meeting, and are relieved at the climax as the tensions are resolved. In fact, the reader's enjoyment is heightened by knowledge not shared by all the characters: we know who this strange official is whose interest in their family is so ominously intense; we know that Joseph's enquiry about Benjamin is enquiry about his full brother, that his concern for their father is concern for his as well. Only the reader can participate with Joseph in the irony of the brothers' self-incrimination in the presence of the one they so wronged and who is now in such complete control of them. Furthermore, the author demonstrates a fine awareness of and hold on the emotional reactions of the reader; we recall, for example, how he prolongs suspension when Joseph is summoned from prison and we are made to wait through a second telling of the Pharaoh's dreams before we find out if

Joseph will succeed in their interpretation after all the wise men of
Egypt have failed. In this case narrative pace is retarded to hold the
reader in suspense; later in ch. 41 the narrative pace is retarded
again, this time to allow the reader to savor Joseph's triumph as a
detailed recital is given of the honors, awards, and titles heaped upon
him. At other points, as when Joseph deals with a famine or arranges
for his family to come to Egypt, the narrative moves with sharp
dispatch.

In all this the novella seeks to reflect life, to present the truth in
life, not what happened once in the past, but what happens. This is
how people act, and will again and again. Not all families are so self-
cursed, but the potential is there in all and too often is realized. Life
is like this, the author wishes to say. People behave like this in these
circumstances, and these are the results. There is an element of
chance in the story, especially in the remarkable rise of Joseph in a
single day (and at this point the novella shares characteristics of the
fairy tale) or the extreme unlikelihood of a small band of starving
Asiatics meeting with the Vizier of Egypt. Yet the unexpected does
happen, for good or ill, in life, and the matter of fundamental concern
is how these characters respond to it. The events of the story are set
on a scale larger than most of life; the stage is more vast than that on
which most of us play out our roles. This simply serves, however, to
magnify life and show all of us more fully and clearly what life is
really like.

There may be lessons for the reader as well, even a moral to the
novella. Certain types of behavior are shown to bring certain results;
patterns become apparent. Unwise love can only sow discord;
vengeance sometimes recoils back on the one who seeks it; deceit
comes to haunt the deceiver; power can easily be abused; risking
one's life for another can bring life and peace to all. Larger patterns
inform the novella. Joseph's brothers do indeed bow down before him
as his dreams foretold (42.6, 9; 50.18). Joseph's remarks to his
brothers when he first reveals his identity and again as he reassures
them after Jacob's death point to a hidden and unobtrusive divine
pattern operating in the course of human events (45.5; 50.20).
However, it is a providential ordering of the course of events that
permits freedom, within limits, for human decisions and actions as
well as rsponsibility for both. Expression is given to limits placed on
human initiative (50.21). We are not gods and can only cause havoc
when we believe and act as if such power were ours.[10] These and

other lessons are to be gained from this novella, and they are underscored in some cases (42.9; 45.5; 50.19-20). But they are not preached in a heavy-handed manner. The story is generally told on its own human terms as the events flow into and out of each other with little overt comment from the author (an exception being the several notices that 'Yahweh was with Joseph' in ch. 39). This is a story that holds itself up to the test of truth, truth in life, and final judgment as to its success is left to each reader.

h. *Setting in Life*

It is not possible to define with as much precision the life setting of the novella as it is with more restricted genres such as the hymn, wedding song, work song, or the priest's blessing. Broadly, the novella is a consciously crafted piece of literary artistry composed by a single author for the reading enjoyment and edification of others. The novella therefore presupposes a literate audience, a level in society with the ability, leisure, and interest to enjoy a work of this type. In the case of the Joseph novella middle to upper class circles in the royal establishment of King Solomon, especially those broadly within the effective reach of court schools in Jerusalem, have been proposed as the audience for which it was first composed. In this regard, in fact, we can suggest that the novella has historical value in that it reveals the literary tastes and styles of the period in which it was produced, as well as broad concerns faced by circles in that world. The Joseph novella may tell us very little about the forefathers of Israel; it can reveal much about the tastes, concerns, and the new literary forms of Solomonic Jerusalem.

In time this novella was taken up into the larger Pentateuchal narrative, possibly in a revision of the Yahwist's epic, to provide an extended transition between major themes in that work. In this context it has taken on added functions, has received additional material (Gen 38, 49, and possibly parts of Gen 48), and attained new links with Israel's ancient traditions about its ancestors. Yet even in this context it stands apart as a clearly distinct type of material. And as such it has continued to entertain and edify its readers as the premier example of the genre novella in the Old Testament.

8

THE STORY OF ESTHER AND MORDECAI
AN EARLY JEWISH NOVELLA

W. Lee Humphreys

The descriptive analysis of the genre novella presented in the previous essay leaves us with the question, 'So what?' What difference does analysis of this type make? The question is appropriate and must not be lost sight of by those engaged in critical study of the Hebrew Bible. For the ultimate pay-off of such analysis can only be a heightened enjoyment and appreciation of the literature of the Old Testament. Only as an author's skills and intentions become manifest and we enter into the dynamics of a work, to be entertained and provoked by it, can genre analysis be judged finally successful. It is as we are directed to the essential features of a literary work and the work allowed to stand for what it is, as features and issues not germane to it are prevented from skewing our perspective, that we are well served by critical study of the Bible. It is to a broad test on these grounds that this essay will submit the analysis presented in the last chapter.

In the previous essay the Joseph novella of Genesis informed our discussion by providing illustrative material. In treatment of the Old Testament novella the Joseph narrative is universally singled out as most typical, sometimes, indeed, as the only instance of this genre in the Hebrew Bible. In this essay we will direct our attention to the story of Esther and Mordecai, offering it as another example of Old Testament novella, and demonstrating how an analysis of it in the terms set out as constitutive of novella heightens our enjoyment and appreciation of it.

1. *The Story of Esther and Mordecai and the Book of Esther*

We have spoken of the *story* of Esther and Mordecai rather than the

Book of Esther. This distinction calls for some comment. We discovered in the previous essay that the Joseph novella underwent further development and reutilization in the course of its preservation in the Hebraic tradition. Materials originally extraneous to it were added, especially at the conclusion, as it was incorporated into the larger narrative framework of the Pentateuch to serve as a transition between the patriarchs of Genesis and the themes of bondage and freedom of Exodus. So too, an older story of Esther and Mordecai underwent further development in assuming the present shape the Book of Esther now has.[1] It is often suggested that the ties binding the story with the Jewish festival of Purim are secondary. As it now stands the story serves as the festal legend for this popular semi-religious celebration of the deliverance of eastern Jews from a pogrom. The links between the story and the feast are two-fold. (1) In an isolated notice it is said that Haman cast the lot (*pûr*, a rare term in Hebrew that the text must itself define by the regular term *gôrāl*) to determine the date for his planned pogrom, hence the name *Purim*. (2) In ch. 9 extensive instructions are issued on precisely when and how Jews are to commemorate their deliverance from annihilation, and some of this material interrupts the natural flow of the narrative as a good story gets bogged down in detail.[2] These links are often assessed as tenuous, suggesting that a once independent story was later utilized to provide justification for the celebration of a festival of possible Persian origin that had become popular in Jewish communities in the eastern diaspora. Such secondary legitimization of a festival already enjoyed by many is not unusual in the history of either Judaism or Christianity. The final result of this is the book as now formed.

These later developments in the story of Esther and Mordecai have accentuated certain elements subdued in the earlier story and have imparted to the Book of Esther a tone of harsh vengeance and ruthless destruction of one's enemies that has appalled some later readers. Martin Luther's comments capture the feelings of many: 'I am so hostile to this book (2 Maccabees) and to Esther that I could wish they did not exist at all; for they judaize too greatly and have much pagan impropriety'.[3] Not all have agreed with Luther's assessment, but the history of the book's difficulties in finding acceptance in the Jewish and Christian canons bespeaks difficulties early readers had with the book in its present form.[4] Other related objections have been raised as well. Much in the book strains historical credibility to the limits and even beyond. Furthermore, standard elements on Jewish religious piety are absent. God is not even mentioned directly in the book![5] This combination of factors has given the Book of Esther a low rating in some circles, a rating only partly neutralized by the high esteem in which it is held by others, for example, the great twelfth-century Jewish scholar Maimonides.

On another level, however, the story of Esther and Mordecai remained always popular, precisely because it is a well-told story. It is a delight! This essential aspect of the story can come into proper focus, and other factors that have led to derogatory assessments can be placed in a legitimately more limited perspective by means of an analysis of the story as a novella. Not all issues can be resolved nor all elements found unsavory removed. Analysis of the story of Esther and Mordecai will not remove all the problems raised by the Book of Esther, but it will cast new light on them, place them in proper perspective, and thereby open for us both the story and the book, allowing us to enjoy and appreciate a distinct example of literary craftsmanship. If so, a barely tolerated stepchild can assume a proud and proper place in the family of biblical literature.

2. Analysis of the Story of Esther and Mordecai as Novella

a. Setting—Time and Place

The story is set in the royal court of a Persian king called Ahasuerus. The action takes place for the most part in the capital city of Susa. One of the functions of the opening chapter is to set the stage, and this is accomplished with a broad brush and rich palette. The occasion is a royal festival that was to last half a year. As a part of the festival the king displayed the extreme wealth and stature that could come only to one whose empire ranged from India to Ethiopia and contained over one hundred and twenty-seven provinces. Everything is on a grandiose scale. The court and its appointments depict a setting of unlimited wealth, and they are described in loving detail. The author shows no restraint in his lavish descriptions, and no restraints were placed on the festival either. Food and especially drink were available in unlimited supply, the latter served in gold vessels, no two alike (according to one possible translation of Est 1.8 the wine was consumed by flagons). And, as we shall see, there were no restraints on the pride and boasting of the king. All power seems to be his to employ as he wishes; the world is at his beck and call.

From the outset the reader of this story is transported into a world that cannot fail to fascinate, a captivating world of wealth, the center of a vast empire, the locus of all earthly power. The setting is designed to grasp the intense interest of readers both ancient and modern, for men and women have always been drawn to accounts of intrigue in high places, be it the ancient court of an Oriental potentate, the court of Russian Czars, or the corridors of power in Washington, D.C. In these contexts power is to be had and used, and with it great wealth and honor. Power, wealth, and honor, and all ultimately in the hands of one man, the king, who by a nod, by a moment's favorable recognition, can elevate for a person the wildest dreams, but one who can, in an instant, crush all hope and life itself. It is a setting in which power, wealth, and honor are to be seized, and in which there are no rules governing the taking and exercise of them except the whim and favor of the king. The one who has the ear of the ruler, the one whom the king trusts, can seize all life has to offer. The loss of royal recognition can destroy careers and blot out life in an instant. In this setting the deepest schemes and passions of men and women will be exposed, as will their priorities and the mainsprings of their lifes. It is a setting designed to reveal the essence of human life, a setting in which the risks are huge and the prizes larger than life itself. We are taken into a world like that woven later by Shahrizad in the *Book of the Thousand Nights and a Night*.

Throughout the narrative we are reminded again and again of this setting. The sumptuous royal harem with its one year long regimen of preparation for its new members (2.12-14), the ease by which maidens can be gathered (2.8) or edicts sent from one end of the empire to the other in all languages (1.22; 3.12-15; 8.13), the ever-ready eunuch in attendance to answer every royal wish (2.8-9; 4.4-9; 7.9), the rewards awaiting those who serve the ruler (6.7-11) and the summary justice awaiting all who fall from grace (7.10), the lavish feasts that punctuate[6] the narrative (1; 2.18; 3.15; 8.17), all run like a golden thread through the rich tapestry of this story.

The time frame is by contrast rather constricted. From beginning to end less than two years pass, and much of it in the opening scenes as the royal feasts run their courses and as those brought for the royal beauty contest are put through their preparation. Once the story is clearly underway the events cover but a brief span of time. Throughout, the looming threat of Haman's pogrom keeps the tension on a thin edge. Critical episodes that form the core of the narrative—from Esther's appearance before the king unsummoned to the death of Haman—are restricted to two event-filled days. More precise denotations of time appear in Esther's three days of fasting and the determination of the date for Haman's pogrom. There is also a concern for the precise fixing of the day(s) for Jewish revenge and its celebration at the conclusion (in material that may well be secondary additions to the story).

b. *Plot*

The story of Esther and Mordecai is a delightfully well-told prose narrative. Against a backdrop so lavish and yet so ominous, a plot unfolds that can only be judged a gem of literary composition. It is in this realm perhaps that the genius of the author is best revealed. It forms a tightly woven fabric of interlocking scenes, laced with irony, building to a climax through action that is fast-paced when necessary and retarded when dramatic effect is best served.

The opening scene is a small gem in itself. Not only does it masterfully set the lavish stage with broad and rich strokes, but it brings the first note of tension into the story. In this scene of unrestraint, where every whim and desire is to be fulfilled in an instant, the whim of the man who should be least restrained is thwarted. The king's command goes forth when he is mellowed by wine that Queen Vashti be brought to display before his courtiers the beauty of the royal consort. She refuses! In an instant the kingdom is set head over heels. Can it be that there are restraints on royal power? Even worse, could these restraints become models for limits on the power of men throughout the empire over their wives? Decisive action is needed and is taken to meet the crisis: Vashti is banished and edicts to all parts of the empire are sent commanding wifely respect for their lords, whatever language the latter may speak. T.H. Gaster has suggested that we have here an ancient harem tale and early piece of women's liberation polemic: one forward woman can set an empire full of men into frantic action to reassert masculine authority, and all the forces of state are called upon to put this female in her 'place'.[7]

What may once have been a brief and distinct harem tale now opens the larger story. The stage is set, and a tension is insinuated through the assertion of royal power and possible restraints on it. A second tension enters the story as well, one that is resolved with little delay. A vacancy in the king's household needs to be filled—the king needs a new queen. A net is cast to gather all virgins in the empire to Susa for preparation for their royal audition, and Esther, the adopted daughter of a Jewish courtier named Mordecai, is caught up in it. Winning the favor of all who come into contact with her, from the eunuch in whose hands she is first placed to the king into whose chambers she finally goes, she becomes queen. Mordecai, who has instructed Esther to keep secret her Jewish identity, is kept before us as we are told how he uncovered a plot to assassinate the king, an event duly recorded in the royal Book of the Chronicles (2.19-23). This last is soon forgotten as the pace of the story now quickens.

Just as the second tension caused by the banishment of Vashti is resolved, another arises that will become the focus of the story, a tension related to that insinuated in ch. 1. It has to do with the use and misuse of unrestrained power. Haman, a royal favorite, is elevated to a position above all other officials; all must now bow down to him. Mordecai refuses to do so, and Haman's rage is such that he vows to destroy not just Mordecai but all his people. The day is determined for the empire-wide pogrom, and royal permission is secured. However, deliverance seems at hand. Mordecai declares to Esther that she must come to the aid of her people in this time of crisis. But there is a complication: Esther has not been summoned to the king's presence for thirty days, and it is a capital offence to appear before him unsummoned. Mordecai is adamant, and Esther finally agrees to take the risk. After three days of fasting she appears at the entrance of the throne room attired in her finest. She is favorably received by the king, and it seems that the means for resolution of the tension is at hand after all. In fact, the king agrees to grant any request she might make. Immediately a further complication occurs, for she simply invites the king and Haman to an intimate soiree she will host that evening. Has she some scheme in mind, or is this just further indication of the high stature of Haman? The reader is puzzled all the more when once again that evening the king, mellowed with wine, renews his offer to grant any request she might make. She simply invites the two men to a similar event the next evening. At the very least Esther is tempting fate.

Haman boasts of his latest triumph to his wife and friends, only to remark further that even this sours before Mordecai's continued stubbornness. His friends suggest that in the light of his apparently unlimited power he simply dispose of Mordecai that very evening. Preparations are made—a gallows seventy-five feet high is erected, and Haman sets out for the palace to secure the king's permission to hang Mordecai. Complications pile up as it appears that Esther's delay in confronting the king with the danger facing the Jews will cost Mordecai his life. Has she toyed with fate too long?

At this point the author calls up all his narrative skills as his plot literally thickens. On the very night that Haman was boasting to his friends and making his preparations to dispose of Mordecai, the king suffered from insomnia and ordered that the Book of the Chronicles be read to him. The incident in which Mordecai uncovered a plot against the king, by now relegated to the very back of the reader's memory, is recalled, and it is noted that Mordecai was never rewarded. This oversight alarms the king, and he seeks immediately to correct it. Needing advice, he is informed that, as luck would have it, Haman, his favored courtier, has entered the palace. Haman is summoned without delay, and the king asks, 'What shall be done for the man whom the king delights to honor?' Haman makes a fatal error, and the reader's delight can hardly be contained as he describes just what he would wish for himself.
Instead he is told,

> 'Do so for Mordecai the Jew . . . '
> So Haman took the robes and the horse, and he arrayed Mordecai and made him ride through the open square of the city, proclaiming, 'Thus shall be done to the man whom the king delights to honor' (Est 6.10-11).

In one sentence, one verse of the text, the fall of Haman is brought about. Yet all the details are now left to the reader's imagination. Only an author with a sure hand and confidence in his reader would allow this climax in the bitter relationship between his two protagonists to pass with so few words and leave so much to the audience. A skilled author knows when not to say too much.

At this point the resolution runs its course with an ever-faster pace. Haman's delight having turned suddenly to lament, his wife and friends can only reinforce his despair. But perhaps the day is not a total disaster; there is still the evening's engagement with Esther and the king. Furthermore the date for the pogrom is still set and fixed in immutable law. Hastened to the meal, Haman finds his fate sealed as the king repeats his earlier offer to Esther, and this time she seizes the chance. Pleading for his life Haman is found compromised by the king and accused—and it is a delightful irony that this time the accusation is false—as assaulting the queen. Haman stands condemned as the timely entrance of the faithful eunuch (was this planned beforehand?) brings to the king's attention the gallows constructed for Mordecai. Haman is hanged without delay.

With Esther's aid Mordecai takes the estate and office of his rival, and from this position of authority the two plan means of thwarting the pogrom. The final danger to the Jews that briefly outlived even Haman himself is overcome. Jews are permitted to defend themselves against all threats by a second immutable decree, and such awe of them falls on the people that many come over to them while all who seek to harm them are destroyed. A final notice regarding Mordecai's high standing with both king and kinfolk fittingly concludes the novella. The complications have been removed, and the tensions have all been resolved. Restraints on the misuse of power have checked its potential for havoc, and an appropriate punishment has fallen on the one who would abuse it.

c. *Narrative Technique*

Scholars have suggested that behind the story of Esther and Mordecai as now formed distinct sources are apparent that were used in its composition. Not only was the story of Vashti once a separate piece, but distinct accounts of Esther and of Mordecai have served as sources for the novella. These have been artfully joined, leaving but traces of their distinctness in the presence of sets of pairs in the text and a few uneven seams (for example, the notice that Mordecai informed Esther of the plot against the king and that she informed him without her relationship to Mordecai being discovered; the awkward 'second time' of 2.19). This is possible, but it must be stressed that any sources utilized were taken up in a most creative way and were so essentially integrated by a skilled narrative hand that those dealing with Esther and Mordecai cannot be disentangled. Even the opening scene is skillfully used to set the stage, form a mood, and introduce an over-arching tension concerning restraint on the abuse of power. We clearly have here the work of one who was more than an editor, one who deserves the title of author.

As we have already noted, the author is a master of narrative pace.

The opening scene along with ch. 2 move slowly enough to allow us to savor the lavish setting and delight in the seeming good fortune of Esther and Mordecai. The pace quickens as the basic tension posed by Haman's pogrom is set out and each seeming resolution brings only new complications. A whole series of finely tuned and interwoven scenes carries the plot at this point, and earlier isolated notices and events are caught up as well (2.10, 19-23). At the climax the narrative hastens to describe the downfall of the villain, as the author demonstrates his ability to set the climax and leave its actual working out to the reader's imagination (6.11). Only with the final edicts issued to thwart the pogrom does the pace slacken as the reader is allowed to savor the success of heroine and hero.

A fine sence of irony and of balance informs the story. Vashti's disobedience results in her fall (1.19); Esther's results in her success (5.1-3). Mordecai uncovers a plot and saves the king (2.19-23); the king unwittingly abets a plot to destroy Mordecai (3.8-15). Mordecai disobeys a direct command from the king (3.2) and survives; Haman obeys a direct command (6.10) to his humiliation. Haman must honor his rival and erect his own gallows. Banquets punctuate the story, opening the narrative, celebrating Esther's triumph as she becomes queen, staging Haman's fall, and celebrating the Jew's deliverance (2.18; 7.1-2; 8.17). Royal edicts are issued first commanding the pogrom and then in perfect balance thwarting it. Haman's fall nicely parallels Mordecai's rise. A clear vision of retributive justice informs the novella.[8]

d. *Characterization*

An essential quality of the novella, shared with the novel, is the depiction of the evolution of the central characters, the charting of their growth and/or disintegration. In the Joseph narrative a complex set of distinct figures evolves in the course of the story, figures drawn remarkably true to life and engaging both the sympathy and the condemnation of the reader, figures often drawn in muted shades. By contrast with these figures, the four central characters in the story of Esther and Mordecai seem more stereotypical, etched in sharp black and white. Generally the figures are seen from the outside as their actions are described; rarely are we given access to their deeper emotions. And yet all four appear to evolve, even if our final judgment must be that the skill of this author expressed itself more in plot formation than in subtle characterization.

Esther first appears as passive and obedient, more acted upon than actor. Caught up in the search for a new queen, she is dutifully obedient to the charge of Mordecai that she keep her Jewishness secret and shrewdly submissive to the advice of Hegai, the eunuch in charge of the king's women, who, no doubt, knows best the royal tastes in such matters. She also serves as the channel by which Mordecai communicates his discovery of the plot against the king. Her own first words are not actually reported until she is urged by Mordecai to intercede on behalf of her people, and they are words of demurral, stressing her helplessness (4.11). So much has happened to Esther without one word from her. To this point she has been the object of most verbs. But at Mordecai's further urging a dramatic change takes place, for her next direct statement is one of determination to act in the face of danger and contains orders on how to set a plan in motion (4.16). From this point on she is a shrewd and able figure, initiating the action, able to execute her plans, obtain royal favor, and defeat her people's enemy, all the while playing a dangerous waiting game that might have resulted in the early death of Mordecai. At the climax it is Esther who transfers Haman's estate to Mordecai and arranges his promotion as well as effects with him (8.3) the salvation of her people. At the outset her hesitancy compounds the danger faced by her people; later she seems dangerously over-confident in her delay in revealing the danger to the king, and Mordecai is almost lost.

A nice balance obtains between the figure of Esther and that of Mordecai. As she becomes more active, he becomes passive. At the outset he is the initiator and controlling force in her life, telling her to keep her religious identity secret, urging her to act to save her people. He even saves the king's life. It is, in fact, the willful refusal of Mordecai to obey the king's command and bow down before Haman that sparks the central tension of the narrative, a refusal on his part that is never fully explained and may have little more behind it than rivalry between courtiers for position and power. Then, at the moment at which Esther acts, he becomes simply the executor of her wishes (4.17). Afterwards, he seems largely to depart from the scene, appearing only as still unrepentant before Haman (5.9) and thus the object of his rage (5.13-14) and unintended homage (6.11). Mordecai now becomes the one acted upon, otherwise returning to the gate to await the outcome of initiatives that have passed into other hands (6.12). He acts again only in concert with Esther to blunt the pogrom through his letters and edicts. The figure of Mordecai seems to envelop that of Esther: he first appears as her protector and adopted father (2.5-7) and then joins her again in the resolution. In fact, the last notice of the narrative deals with Mordecai (10.1-3). He is first seen as a royal official serving his king, and he is again found at the end in royal service.

Over against the hero and heroine stands the villain Haman. Seemingly so much in control of events, able to mold them to fit his purposes, he is in time overrun by the course of the narrative, and when he finally realizes this, he is on a downward plunge that cannot be reversed. Both coincidence and Esther nicely set him up for a fall, and his fall is as total as befits this archetypical villain. It is of interest that he is the one figure whose emotions, feelings, and motives are related in any detail. The reader is told of his rage at Mordecai's early refusal to acknowledge him (3.5-6), of the bitterness that its continuance provokes (5.9, 13), of his pride (5.9, 12), and of his terror when exposed by Esther (7.6). His deepest thoughts are related at the moment when the king seeks his advice: 'Whom would the king delight to honor more than me?' In his moment of folly, in his failure to divine correctly the nature of the situation confronting him, he lends an active hand to the determination of his future. He believes he is in control and able to rid himself of a bitter thorn in his life, only to fix for himself a fate he did not intend. He even built his own gallows (7.9). This range of emotions, from proud confidence through humiliation to stark terror is allowed no other figure in the story. Only in a final brief declarative sentence (7.10) are we distanced from him as he is led to his death. His face is covered, and the author seems to be asking the reader's own imagination to supply his last bitter taste of irony laced with terror.

The remaining central character is the king, a figure in whom all power resides and yet who seems so unable to exercise it other than in unthinking bursts of activity. On a whim he summons Vashti to display her beauty and is thwarted. In anger he banishes her and then laments her absence. On the spur of the moment, it seems, he elevates Haman and quickly gives in to his request to destroy the Jews without investigation of the situation or even much thought. Thought, foresight, care in planning just are not in his character. He greets the unsummoned Esther with a gracious but rash 'What is your request? It shall be given you, even to half my kingdom', and repeats this twice when influenced by wine (5.6; 7.2). Wine seems especially to trigger the spontaneous in him (1.10). And when he learns the full dimensions of Haman's villainy he rushes from the scene in a rage. All power is his, and he can exercise it only in unthinking bursts of passion or desire, bursts upon which hang, however, the fate of many. Beyond this he is strangely malleable, bent first by Haman to further his schemes and then by Esther to undo the damage caused. Only once does he seek advice, and then the results are creative: learning that Mordecai had not been rewarded for former service, he seeks counsel. In this case it is the calculating Haman who proves to be foolishly thoughtless. It is this spontaneity and the malleability of the king that prevents him from appearing a villain like Haman. He is passionate and thoughtless at points, but never the calculating manipulater in the manner of Haman. We even tend to sympathize with the poor dolt, especially as in the resolution he shows that his heart is in the right place. Ironically, the only point at which it is possible to feel any sympathy for Haman is at the point at which he acts without thought and stages his own humiliation.

e. *The Novella as Fiction*

In the story of Esther and Mordecai we have a narrative so well told that the question as to whether these things actually happened slips from our concern in the sheer enjoyment of it. And our assessment of the story as a novella suggests that this is appropriate. Attempts to defend the essential historicity of the material have been quite unsuccessful when judged by any reasonable standards of historical inquiry.[9] This is not to deny that the author of the story had and utilized a reasonably exact knowledge of the general course of Persian history and especially of life in its royal court. The setting of the story imparts to it a high degree of verisimilitude, even with regard to the extensive feasting and wealth of the palace. Ahasuerus is generally identified as Xerxes I (485-465 BC) and is the only demonstrable historical figure in the material. But from what we know of his reign there is no direct confirmation of the events of our story, even if they seem broadly in line with the character and rule of this fourth Persian king. The author is careful to set his story with some exactness in time and place, but is also willing to exploit the fabulous potential of that era and setting for his own narrative purposes. It is true that the name Mordecai (in the form Marduka) has appeared in Aramaic documents from the period, even that an official with that name is mentioned in a document that dates near the outset of Xerxes' reign. However, no information is given about that figure that would clearly link him with the Mordecai of the story, and we have no way of knowing how common names like his and Esther's were at that time (both are built upon the names of the Babylonian deities Marduk and Ishtar).

Beyond this there are some distinct improbabilities in the story. The statement that Mordecai was part of the first deportation from Jerusalem in 598/7 would make him and Esther far too old for participation in events of this sort set in the reign of Xerxes I over a century later. Esther would not have caught even the king's eye! The Greek historian Herodotus tells us that Persian queens were selected from a restricted group of seven noble families, a fact that would disqualify Esther, whatever her other qualifications. Herodotus also places Xerxes away fighting Greece in the early period of his rule, the period in which our story is set, and he further states that one Amestris was queen during the period assigned to Esther (Est 2.6; 3.7—the seventh through twelfth years of Xerxes). Of course, these could be the type of errors to which even historians are prone, and it is possible that Herodotus is not to be trusted. But other improbabilities stretch the credulity of the reader as well, even as they add greatly to the dramatic effect and appeal of the story and are in some cases integral to its development. The immutable 'law of the Medes and Persians' (1.19; 8.8; 9.27; Dan 6.8, 9, 15) would be the type of barrier to effective rule that no absolute monarch would allow, and laws demanding that all men be lords of their homes, edicts allowing the slaughter of vast numbers of one's subjects and announced publicly months before the event, further edicts permitting fighting throughout the kingdom and even in the palace itself, are all well beyond the probable if not wholly into the impossible. Yet it must also be noted that just these features serve to heighten the tension in the story and are essential to its development.[10] All this, along with the lack of external verification for any part of the story, frustrates attempts to place the story of Esther and Mordecai firmly within the sphere of the historical, and it reinforces the impression already gained from our analysis of plot, narrative techniques, and characterization that we have before us an artfully conceived and executed product of a very creative imagination.

The Book of Esther has been called a 'historical novel' (we might suggest 'novella'), and one appraisal of it went on to say that elements of 'comparison with a pearl are possible. A lustrous pearl consists of a hard core of sand around which successive layers of colorful foreign substance have accumulated.'[11] To this we would only add that the value of a pearl, as well as the pleasure it gives, lies just in those lustrous layers of 'foreign substance' and not in a rude grain of coarse sand so fully and successfully buried beneath them. To strip the layers formed to protect the oyster from the coarse grain is to destroy a pearl, and a fine novella as well. The possibility of a historical core cannot be denied, but it is the author's creative building about it a story rich in imagination and ripe for enjoyment that must first concern us.

f. *Intent*

We have suggested that the author of a novella seeks both to entertain and to submit his work to the test of truth in life. Clearly the story of Esther and Mordecai entertains; the reader is delighted by a carefully constructed plot in which complications are set forth and apparently resolved only to reveal other and deeper complications. And when the final resolution is attained, and Esther, Mordecai, and their fellow Jews are delivered, the reader has been taken through an emotional maze from suspense through fear and on to relief. The skill and narrative techniques employed in this have been suggested above.

Can we say that this novella passes the test of truth in life? Is this the way life is? We have noted that the novella does not report what happened but what happens, and it is in these terms that we must assess this novella as well. Certainly few in life either reach the heights attained by Esther and Mordecai or live in such lavish surroundings. Few as well face such immediate danger in that setting or are ever caught up in such a web of mortal intrigue. Few villains will ever be met as unqualifiedly evil as Haman. In this regard the figures are larger than life and stride across a stage larger than that on which most of us will play our parts. But this magnification of life may well serve to expose its core all the more clearly.

The author seems to assert that the unexpected is clearly a part of life. Fortuitous events do take place. Esther is caught up in a search for a queen; royal insomnia averts the hanging of Mordecai. Throughout, events are triggered by the impulse of a ruler quite subject to the power of wine (see also 3.15). But the unexpected, the fortuitous, must be seized if its potential is to be realized. Esther wisely places herself in the care of the very official who would know best the king's taste; in the contest she obtains inside help (2.15). After initial reluctance she uses her new position to stop Haman, even if she tempts fate in the process. And therein lies a lesson as well. Had the king slept that fateful night Mordecai would have surely been hanged before the second evening's dinner. The result was to make Haman's fall all the more dramatic and complete. But even the best efforts can fail without an element of luck. Perhaps the author is suggesting that it is possible for even the best of us—Esther as well as Haman—to over-estimate our potential to control a situation and effect what we intend. Human beings exercise a significant degree of control over their destinies, but they are also caught up in a nexus of human relations in which decisions and events, often quite distant, profoundly alter their lives. A wife's disobedience, a courtier's refusal to pay homage to a rival, both set in motion a pattern of events that move far beyond the initial situation.

It is well known and often noted that the Book of Esther makes no mention of the deity.[12] Indeed, the story moves on the very human level of court intrigue and the struggle for position, power, honor, and riches. Finely tuned coincidences do occur; the *deus ex machina* does not. Human beings struggle and their skill and goodness, mixed with luck, bring success or failure. Haman in a critical moment proves to be a fool, and in a situation filled with danger is blind to the possibilities it holds—'Whom would the king delight to honor more than me?' Esther, in a situation demanding choice, first holds back and, only when urged, acts with a clear sense of her limits and the risks involved—'Then I will go to the king, though it is against the law; and if I perish, I perish'. Yet, in the very words used by Mordecai to urge her to act many find a hidden reference to the providential hand of the deity:

> For if you keep silence at such a time as this, relief and deliverance will rise for the Jews from another quarter ... And who knows whether you have not come to the kingdom for such a time as this? (Est 4.14).

The point is not labored, however. Yet it would seem likely that a Jewish reader steeped in the Hebraic heritage would be alert to the quiet hand of providence informing the narrative, and would set the coincidences in just this light. Human freedom to effect one's own life and human responsibility for the results are not denied. But human beings live on a stage that is larger and more complex than their own making. Further, the author suggests that it is a stage designed to encourage goodness, to frustrate evil in the end, and to preserve justice and order in the world.[13]

Beyond this the author seeks to assert to the reader that it is possible for Jews in the diaspora to live full and effective lives in a world that at times is alien and threatening, but is ultimately hospitable. There will be men like Haman in it—the dangers are real—and there will be dolts in positions of great power. But as a representative of the world the king is not inherently evil. He intends to do good, and the final notice of the story sets the welfare of the king and state in harmony with that of the Jews and especially the hero and heroine. A pattern for Jewish life is here implied that in no way restricts full and effective engagement with the rich and rewarding life in the larger world in which diaspora Jews found themselves.[14]

g. *Setting in Life*

In this last observation we have already touched on the life setting for the story of Esther and Mordecai. It served to entertain Jews in the eastern diaspora during the late Persian and early Hellenistic periods.[15] It addressed a literate audience whose exposure to the royal court, however distant it was from their daily lives, was enough that they would be caught up in a story of intrigue and power set there. It addressed Jews who struggled to live and define a style of life in diaspora, in a world in which they were a minority, but a world that held out to them possibilities for rewarding and creative lives even as it held out dangers as well. The latter are real enough, but they are not essentially constitutive of that world (contrast the depiction of the pagan world in the visions in Dan 7–12). Beyond this it is difficult to specify a life setting for the story except to note that it became widely popular throughout diaspora Jewish communities.

The Book of Esther as now formed and set in Jewish tradition has, however, a more specific setting in life. It serves as the festal legend for Purim and is still read in conjunction with that celebration each year. We have suggested that this connection is secondary, a reflection of a later use of a story that in origin had no such links. This later utilization quite possibly brought into the story some additions, especially in the somewhat heavy-handed material dealing with the date and manner of celebration of the feast found in ch. 9. Purim was and remains a popular festival, a time for unrestrained celebration with both food and drink (if not quite to the excess of Ahasuerus in ch. 1), and it is often the custom to enact the story in childrens' pageants. This further insured the continued preservation of a story whose artful composition would probably have been enough to make certain its continued popularity. In time, as noted, additions were made to the story (the Additions to Esther found in the Jewish and Protestant Apocrypha) that altered its character in fundamental ways. Beyond even this the book has gathered about it a body of legendary lore as rich and full as any unit of similar size in the Hebrew Bible. All this serves to demonstrate how this book continued to spark the imaginations of Jews and bears further witness to the fact that, in spite of extended debate about its fitness for the canon of Scripture, a well crafted story will always find readers to delight.

9

FABLE

Ann M. Vater Solomon

Stories of talking plants and animals are always fascinating to human audiences. These tales with their aura of unreality allow the story-teller unusual opportunities for explaining characteristics of the flora or fauna, teaching some kind of moral, or satirizing human society. In the Hebrew Scriptures there are a variety of such animal or plant stories as the fables in Judg 9; 2 Kgs 14; the allegories in Ezek 17; 24; 19; and the parables in Isa 5.1-7; Jer 18.1-11.[1] The purpose of the present chapter is to concentrate upon one type of these tales, the fable. The question of what a fable is, how a story-teller presents one, what affect the story is to have in society, or what truth value the story may have will take us to the boundaries of form criticism itself as it attempts to understand the marvelous elements of storytelling. For the question of how fictional or somehow unreal narrative forms can ring true is of interest to every student of sacred literature. This question can be approached through form criticism, but eventually it broadens onto the horizon of that meaning which allows the touching of separate worlds. Let us begin with analyzing the fable, the marvelous tales where reality and unreality happily coexist.

1. *What is a Fable?*

Most people employ the term 'fable' for a simple fictional story featuring talking animals, told to illustrate some common moral of society, for example Aesop's fable of the tortoise and the hare. Likewise anthropologists frequently use the term 'fable' for a moral animal tale.[2] To do justice, however, to the particular examples of the fable in the Old Testament, it is necessary to define each element of the fable more completely. Jotham's and Jehoash's fables feature talking plants rather than animals, have no explicit moral, and apply to very specific political situations. We will examine the definition once more by looking at (1) a fable's characters; (2) its content; and (3) its context. First, however, let us consider the underlying story form.[3]

Basically a fable is a simple, yet unreal type of story. The English word 'fabulous' carries some of this aura of going beyond normal reality. A fable is simple, that is, it is not very long, and it has only a short plot and few incidents. A fable is a story, that is, a piece of prose told through a sequence of perceptions in time. What makes this short strange story unique, however, are its characters, content, and context.

The characters in a fable are usually animals, but they may be plants or other elements of nature, human-made objects (an axe, a pot), or abstractions (Hunger, Death). Fables may also include humans and, some have argued, the deity as well.[4] However, stories which include the central symbol of one's own religion such as its deity are usually meant to be understood as true in a different sense than a fable and are therefore to be excluded. *Another* society's deity may be included in a fable, illustrating the process which anthropologists have observed in which one group's myths (true, sacred stories) become another group's folktales or vice versa.[5] The main character in a fable, however, is not a person, but a personified reality like an animal or a plant.[6]

By definition, the content of a fable must include some moral observation. This element can be woven into a fable in a variety of ways, either explicitly, implicitly in the plot, or by being presupposed by the plot and characterization. The most obvious fashion is to conclude a fable with a proverb, a short wise saying, such as 'She who laughs last, laughs best'.[7] Alternatively, a rule of behavior can be woven into the plot and need not be stated directly, as in 2 Kgs 14. If desired, the rule could be extracted and put into a proverb like 'A young buck can't stand against a bull'. Or again, satire or other criticism of human society can be worked into a fable through either the plot or the characterization of the animal or plants. In this case, a certain morality is presupposed, and is indirectly reinforced or corrected through criticism, as in Judg 9.

Fables may also contain matters of an aetiological nature, that is, answers to questions about the origin of the ways of nature or society. Some historians of culture think that fables were amoral at first, and then developed their moral content.[8] But anthropologists have observed the great antiquity of the moral element in fables and would classify amoral stories as simply animal or plant tales.[9] As G.E. Lessing observed in the eighteenth century, the fable's most telling characteristic, in addition to its unusual characters, is its moral ingredient.[10]

2. The Societal Context of a Fable

The context, or specific social situation, in which the fable is told and employed is ultimately the deciding factor in refining its genre. The context of a fable includes (1) the type of narrator and audience (from which social groups they come, how public or private is the access to the fable), (2) the purpose and tone of the fable (how narrator and the fable's audience regard the genre itself, and to what social situation it applies), (3) the circumstances of its narration (when and where a fable is told), and (4) the style of narration (narrator's devices and audience participation). These are the factors which are most difficult to reconstruct from a written fable, and so the many disagreements among literary scholars, historians, and religionists over these basic problems is quite understandable.[11] But, since a change in any one of these factors may radically alter the cultural meaning of a genre, we must not avoid a consideration of these factors. Further, in the transition of a genre from oral to written form (and in the history of the transmission of the fable, back to oral form again), it is the change in these factors of the social situation which is most pronounced. Written literature often involves a change of transmitters and audience, of motivation and function. Inevitably it involves some change of when and where a genre is used, and certainly written literature changes the dynamics of narration itself. With no dramatic gestures on the face of the narrator before us, and no songs or voice to provide the rhythm, we must rely upon a range of other literary devices in order to understand a genre.[12]

Now let us examine these important elements of a fable's cultural context. (1) The fable is a highly popular genre, beloved of children and their many teachers. But it may be also much more restricted, in that it is told by political leaders or their critics (like the prophets). (2) When addressing children and most adults, the narrator has teaching or entertainment with a serious purpose in mind, that is, the communication of moral values in order to exercise social control, validate authority, or provide some temporary release from society.[13] But when addressing the power structure in a society, the narrator has political change in mind, and his or her tone becomes satirical. (3) The circumstances of when a fable is told, or when fables are printed, are also two-fold. When a question arises about proper behavior, perhaps with some doubt or dissatisfaction with current attitudes and actions, a particularly entertaining way to answer it is to tell a fable. Collections of such fables are a sort of reference book for children and adults; they are preferably illustrated and contain a wonderful variety of stories. But usually when fables are published, they are presumed to have a political purpose. When the present head or leadership in a society is challenged, fables are more likely to be published, either sent as written messages (2 Kgs 14) or put out as a collection.[14] (4) The style of narration also has a two-fold character, depending upon the two audiences. In the oral telling of fables to children or adults, narrators delight in impersonating the animals, and evoking congenial audience reaction. However, in the written publication of political fables, the narrator probably has a hostile audience, and therefore may be more blunt and direct in the portrayal of characters and the sequence of events. Biblical literature has not preserved any fables from the first context, but only the fable from the satirical political context. Later we shall return to the question of how the choice of characters and the content of the fable have also been influenced by its political context, a question overlooked by previous investigators of the genre.

Now that the common use of the term fable has been expanded with some basic ideas, let us proceed to answer the question of what a fable is by first, investigating the history of the term; secondly, relating the genre to larger and smaller genres; and, thirdly, comparing the genre to similar types like parable and allegory. Although the investigation of etymologies is rightfully suspect at present among certain historical-critical scholars,[15] I wish to explore the terms 'fable' and the Hebrew *māšāl* in order to establish some central ideas about the genre, and to provide the terminology for the subsequent discussion of the relationship between genres.

3. *The History of the Term*

There is no distinct name in the Hebrew of 2 Kgs 14 or Judg 9 for the plant stories. However, it appears that the Israelites had the same name for several genres. The Hebrew word *māšāl* primarily means proverb, but includes within its usage the whole range of allegory, wisdom songs, Balaam's oracles and statements. Four central ideas emerge from the root metaphors and usages of 'fable' and *māšāl*. (i) Both terms seem to be based on the idea of 'words which control behavior'. The proto-Indo-European root of 'fable', from Latin 'fari', is 'bha', 'to speak'—a word whose connotation is most apparent in the English word 'ban'. The verb *māšāl* usually means to rule or have dominion over and when a prophet uses *māšāl* for his 'political' oracle, the question is who rules over Israel.[16] (ii) The 'fable' conveys the idea of an unreal story, particularly in the adjective 'fabled', which means 'fictitious', or the verb 'fabling', to tell falsehoods, although the Latin noun *fabula* simply means a story. (iii) The Latin *fabula* may also mean a conversation, and thus points up a crucial idea for a fable—the necessity of portraying an animal or plant as talking. (iv) The Hebrew noun *māšāl* appears to be derived from a root meaning 'to compare', and therefore reveals the purpose of a fable, to draw some comparison between one kind of reality and another. To summarize, then, an investigation of the words 'fable' and '*mashal*' suggests four important elements in the definition of the genre: the moral purpose—words which control behavior; its fictitious quality; its personification of characters through talking; and its teaching or political functions by drawing comparisions between worlds.

4. *The Relationship of the Fable to other Genres*

The broader English genre of which fables are a part is the story (Lat. *fabula*) or folklore. It is possible to distinguish two categories within these, accounts (myths and legends) and fiction (folktales such as trickster tales, tall tales, fairy tales, animal or plant tales). A fable would then be a type of fiction, the moral animal or plant tale. Anthropologists have noted that societies differ in their categorization, some having one term for all,[17] others differentiating myth-legends from folktales,[18] others setting off myths from all other types.[19] This categorization of fables as a type of fiction, as opposed to myths or legends,[20] raises the question of how it is perceived as true, or how it may function as a religious story. We shall return to this question later in treating the cultural truth of a fable.

A fable may contain smaller genres within it, most characteristic of which are the proverb (the usual meaning of Hebrew *māšāl*), or the conversation (Latin *fabula*). This may either be direct speech or in the form of a message exchange, as in 2 Kgs 14.

Some have defined a fable as a naive form of allegory[21] or as a simple parable.[22] In what sense are these comparison stories related to one another? All these share the form of stories which may be used to criticize society, but parables and allegories admit human beings and the deity into central roles in their stories. They are also subtler forms of teaching values, the parable pointing from one known reality to a more mysterious one, and the allegory drawing direct connections between two whole realms of associations. Parables and allegories also have other didactic functions than teaching morality or expressing satire. They are meant to explore and open up new realities, a new connection between human realities, whereas the fable comes down on questions of morality or politics. Some have argued that the fable precedes the parable or allegory, and that one underlies the others.[23] It may be that a fable underlies Isaiah's parable of the vineyard, although the poet's metaphor of a vineyard arises naturally out of ordinary speech. It is more likely that there is a political fable underlying Ezekiel's allegory of the cypress in ch. 31, for the feeling of satire in a mixture of reality and unreality is very similar to that of the political fable.[24]

In conclusion, the fable may be defined as a simple unreal type of oral or written tale, featuring talking animals or plants, told to reinforce some moral teaching or to satirize political leaders. It is employed in ordinary didactic contexts or in the open political sphere. The political fable is more akin to political allegory in its satirical feelings and mixture of reality and unreality, while the parable points from a human reality to another reality in an aura of mystery.

A full definition of the genre fable would include the examination of a specific example of the telling of a fable, for only then can we appreciate the narrator's art, and get a feeling for the audience's weighing of the various possible elements in a fable, such as entertainment, education, practice in public speaking, humor, ridicule, and moralizing.[25] In the next chapter, on 2 Kgs 14, such an example will be provided. For now, let us at least list some famous examples of the genre fable in both their ordinary moral and political types.

5. *Examples of Moral and Political Fables*

Virtually every Western and pre-literate culture has created fables, and examples of both political fables and ordinary moral fables can be found readily in all of them.[26] In our own time, authors such as James Thurber and George Orwell (*Animal Farm*) represent political fabulists. Ordinary fables are best exemplified in the Brer Rabbit tales, and in some animated cartoons. In the seventeenth and eighteenth centuries famous political fabulists were Jean de la Fontaine (*Roman de Renart*, a sly fox) and Ivan A. Krylo (*Basili*, a collection of fables). In the twelfth century both Marie de France and Christine de Pisan collected beast fables. Marie de France expanded the Biblical fable of Jotham by employing the broomtree, realizing full well its political function.[27] In the sixth century BCE collection of Aesop there are many animal fables, and also stories of the rivalry between trees for leadership.[28] As far back as the third and second millennia BCE, there are Sumerian and Old Babylonian examples of both kinds of fables, the Old Babylonian 'Dispute between the Tamarisk and the Date Palm' being a political type of fable.[29] Hundreds of Indian and African examples of fables demonstrate the prevalence, popularity, and antiquity of this genre in both of its types.

After briefly reviewing the history of the genre fable, we confront the question of whether the author of the Biblical fables borrowed from some adjacent culture. Diffusionist anthropologists in the 1930s and 1940s, as well as historians of an evolutionary frame of mind, would explain many steps in the history of a genre as direct borrowing from one group to another. In his monumental work on folklore, the diffusionist Stith Thompson established hundreds of motifs, some simple ones being found in fables, and showed how the same motif could combine and recombine in many different stories. More recent work in anthropology and history certainly allows for borrowing, but stresses instead the internal social processes which provide the situations out of which genres are born. Certainly the specific plants used in Jotham's and Jehoash's fables dictate a Syro-Palestinian matrix, and the use of plant fables to satirize political leaders is a prevalent phenomenon in many cultures. Let us turn now to a closer examination of the social functions of the political plant fable.

6. *The Social Functions of Fables*

In describing the societal functions of verbal art or folklore, it is possible to differentiate two basic spheres, the social and the political. The ordinary animal fable operates largely in the social sphere, the plant fable largely in the political sphere. That is, the functions of the animal fable tend to be those of (i) education—transmission of knowledge, values and attitudes in order to teach social customs and ethical standards; (ii) social control—construction of a system of rewards with praise, and punishment with criticism or ridicule to regulate behavior; (iii) social authority—providing rationalizations for social institutions and actions; and (iv) socio-pyschological release—allowing fantasies of escape from the accidents of geography, biology or society.[30] All these social functions of a genre stress the stability and continuity of a culture, with the third function of providing explanations for social authority being the primary one of ordinary moral fables. Animal fables are particularly entertaining because they provide some release from the human situation, yet they are understood as immediately applicable to real society in incisive ways.

The fable also can be made to operate in the political sphere of society. Either it provides propaganda in order to consolidate power or else it expresses dissent in a call for political change. The plant fable almost always serves the political functions of challenging leadership or challenging rivals to the power structure. In the two Biblical fables, there is an example of each of the latter type. Jotham's fable in Judg 9 is a satire on kingship itself as a form of governance, while challenging the leadership of Abimelech. Jehoash's fable in 2 Kgs 14 hurls an insulting challenge at the rival to his kingship, Amaziah.

Might there be reasons for the choice of the plant fable to perform these political functions? From a study of anthropological research into the relationship between African visual arts and leadership, I would like to suggest some answers to this question. For it certainly is striking that although animal fables are far more numerous than plant fables, it is precisely in the political sphere that most plant fables operate. In his massive work on the *Science of Folklore* (first published in 1930), Alexander Krappe noted the smaller number of plant fables in the world's folklore, and tried to explain it on the basis of a lack of congeniality to the human condition.

The reason must be sought, I believe, in the strain imposed upon
the imagination when representing plants as walking and acting
and discoursing, a strain far less pronounced, of course, in the case
of the animal fable.[31]

Pet lovers and plant fanciers might wish to debate Krappe's point,
and science fiction fans would wish to add machines to the list of
candidates, but in general, his perception is probably still correct. In
fact, it is exactly this more fantastic quality of plant fables that makes
them better political vehicles in a pre-industrial society. Let us
consider a summary of a study done in Africa on the characteristics
of official art in a variety of societies.

In their very interesting study, *African Art and Leadership*, D.
Fraser and M. Cole outline the structure and function of several
types of visual arts, such as masks and footstools, which are
connected with such types of leadership as kingship, chieftaincy, and
more independent or acephalous forms.[32] Many of these observations
are applicable to the political fable as well. I would like to concentrate
on just two of them. In describing the structure of these art forms,
they state that there is a correlation between naturalism in art and
the type of society whose leader produces the art.

> Least imitative forms, on the whole, are found among such
> segmentary or acephalous peoples as the Lega, Nybaka, or Bobo . . .
> Peoples with chiefs produce a more naturalistic art . . . In court
> styles, naturalism is always blended with idealism.[33]

In recent studies of Israelite religion and society, the period of the
Judges has been understood with the help of the model of the
segmentary or acephalous type of society.[34] Jotham's fable, which is
rather fantastic in its elaborate plant conversations, is less imitative
of reality than Jehoash's, which was produced in a court and given a
more naturalistic turn with the animal who crushes the small plant.
But why the choice of the plant fable for political ends in the first
place?

In listing the functions of African leadership art, Fraser and Cole
stress the importance of leaders first establishing a detached, yet
visible symbol for their own political arena. From this 'other place',
they can then carry on communication in order to regulate, adjudicate,
reward, and edify their constituencies.[35] Plant fables, especially
stories about trees, provide excellent symbolic material for a more
remote yet visible realm, and thus are better adapted to the uses of

political leaders. Jotham's fable even suggests that outstanding figures should not give up their other useful societal functions to concentrate exclusively on single headship. We shall consider in some detail how the form and function of a particular political fable relies upon the type of society involved, just as the initial form and function of a fable depends upon the social context in which it operates.

7. *The Truth of the Fable*

The most intriguing question in genre studies, however, remains to be asked. In what sense is a particular example of a genre true in its own culture? How can stories which contain fiction or some admixture of fact ring true? This is what anthropologists call the cultural context of a genre, by which they mean how a particular verbal art form is related to an audience's understanding of themselves and their world.[36] Anthropologists of religion would then ask further of a fable in a religious context how it relates to the central symbols of the culture and its religious systems, and how it partakes of the natural world.[37] Religionists would go one step further and ask for the true meaning of a particular set of words in relation to various kinds of religious experience. We shall return to these last two questions in discussing Biblical fables of the cedar and the thistle, in regard to the Israelite symbol of kingship for their deity and culture, the meaning of the cedar in their religious imagination, and the various religious perspectives of the two tellers of the fable, the Deuteronomist (2 Kgs 14) and the Chronicler (2 Chr 25). In regard to the first question, however, that of the cultural context of truth for a particular story, it is possible to offer my own modification of some conclusions from William Bascom's work on folklore.

Just as in the operation of societal functions mentioned above, verbal or written art may emphasize either continuity or discontinuity with its own culture. Each of these two realms may be subdivided into the present, past, and future, yielding the following possible relationships between a particular example of a genre and its culture, whether the genre be in the form of fact or fiction, or some combination thereof. In the case of continuity between art and culture, a fable may contain (A-1) some contemporary societal practice; (A-2) some clues to past events or customs; or (A-3) the future goals of a culture. In the realm of discontinuity, a genre may contain (B-1) present forbidden practices; (B-2) entirely earlier stages of culture; or (B-3) compensatory or wish fulfillments. In the moral dimension of the fable, and in other moral genres of verbal and oral literature, there is a further critical realm which emphasizes the relationship between what a good culture might be like and the existing one. (The same might also be argued for the social and political functions noted above.) In the realm of criticism then, a genre may contain (C-1) what the present culture should be; (C-2) what the past might have been, (C-3) what the future could be. Perhaps a good example of the possibilities of meaning which must be considered in attempting to understand another culture would be to ask the meaning of a particular religious law in a given ancient or pre-literate society. How did the people regard it? As reinforcing what they usually did? As already quite removed from their world? Or as challenging them to change? Even in reading the present law code of Britain or France, would an outsider know which laws were actually practiced, which were never meant to be literally enforced, or which represent practical ideals by which to evaluate life? A particular example of a genre then may be true to a culture in many different ways.

The question of the truth of a particular genre is often reduced to the realm of (A), continuity with a culture, and is further shrunk to providing evidence for what actually happened in the past. Fables, a recent author has happily announced, given their fictitious character, 'do not present problems for the historian'.[38] That is, their truth cannot be historical, nor do they have 'historical pretensions',

> even if on a purely theoretical plane the narrative part could contain historical elements when dealing with people.[39]

Another attempt to derive cultural truth from the Biblical fables is represented by those who consider the application of Jotham's fable to Abimelech and Joash's fable to Amaziah as secondary, historicizing developments.[40] Supposedly these fables existed independently at first, completely apart from any political or historical context. That such a situation is highly unlikely can be deduced from the sociological observations above and the following discussion of a particular example of the genre. Rather, this 'historicization' may be a modern commentator's way of stating the truth of the fable.

As suggested in the reflection on Bascom's work above, the question of cultural truth can not be reduced to only 'what events actually happened'. Rather we need the perspective of the story-teller to help us know how to understand the truth of a story. We need to assemble as much knowledge and as many feelings and insights into a culture as possible to answer the question of truth. Jotham's fable, for example, not only characterizes a present choice for leader, Abimelech, as a thorny problem. It also rings true on the level of what the present society should be (without any human king) and who the present king actually is, that is, God. Thus Jotham's fable can be seen as a theocratic satire on the present, a 'present' from the perspective of the Exile (hundreds of years later) by the final storyteller of the book of Judges.

With these descriptions of the societal functions and cultural context of truth of the fable, the political fable in a religious context in particular, we conclude the definition of the genre fable. In doing so, it has been established that there are two different types of fable corresponding to two separate contexts: teaching and power politics, the Old Testament having examples only from the political realm.

10

JEHOASH'S FABLE OF THE THISTLE AND THE CEDAR
(2 Kings 14.8-14 and 2 Chronicles 25.17-24)

Ann M. Vater Solomon

8. Then Amaziah sent messengers to Jehoash, son of Jehoahaz, son of Jehu, king of Israel, saying: 'Come on, let's face each other'. 9. So Jehoash, king of Israel, sent to Amaziah, king of Judah, saying:

> 'The thistle, which was in Lebanon,
> sent to the cedar, which was in Lebanon, saying,
> "Give your daughter to my son for a wife".
> But a beast of the field, which was in Lebanon,
> marched by and trampled down the thistle.'

10. Indeed, you have struck down Edom, and you would raise your sights. Glory in it, but stay at home. For why should you venture into evil, then fall, you and Judah with you?' 11. But Amaziah would not listen. So Jehoash, king of Israel, went up, and he and Amaziah, king of Judah, faced each other at Beth Shemesh, which is in Judah. 12. And Judah was beaten down before Israel, and they fled, each man to his tent.

13. Thus Amaziah, king of Judah, son of Jehoash, son of Ahaziah, seized Jehoash, king of Israel, at Beth Shemesh. As they entered Jerusalem, he broke down the wall of Jerusalem from the gate of Ephraim to the corner gate, four hundred cubits. 14. Taking all the gold and the silver, and all the vessels found in the house of the LORD, and in the treasuries of the house of the king, and even hostages, he returned to Samaria (2 Kgs 14.8-14).

17. After taking counsel, Amaziah, king of Judah, sent to Joash, son of Jehoahaz, son of Jehu, king of Israel, saying, 'You, let's face each other'. 18. So Joash, king of Israel, sent to Amaziah, king of Judah, saying:

'The thistle, which was in Lebanon,
    sent to the cedar, which was in Lebanon, saying,
    "Give your daughter to my son for a wife".
But a beast of the field, which was in Lebanon,
    Marched by and trampled down the thistle.'

19. You say, "Look, you have struck down Edom, and you would raise your sights for glory". Now remain at home. For why should you venture into evil, then fall, you and Judah with you?' 20. But Amaziah would not listen, for the matter was from God, that they might be delivered by hand, because they inquired of the deity of Edom. 21. So Joash, king of Israel, went up, and he and Amaziah, king of Judah, faced each other at Beth Shemesh, which is in Judah. 22. And Judah was beaten down before Israel, and they fled to their tents.

23. Thus Amaziah, king of Judah, son of Joash, son of Jehoahaz, seized Joash, king of Israel, at Beth Shemesh, and he brought him to Jerusalem, and he broke down the wall of Jerusalem from the gate of Ephraim to the facing gate, four hundred cubits. 24. With all the gold and the silver, and all the vessels found in the house of God, with Obed-Edom, and the treasures of the house of the king, and even hostages, he returned to Samaria (2 Chr 25.17-24) (translations mine).

The political fable I have chosen to illustrate the genre 'fable' is embedded in King Jehoash's reply to the challenge of his southern rival, King Amaziah of Judah. The Bible contains two versions of their story, one in 2 Kgs 14 and one in 2 Chr 25. The fable, however, is exactly the same, though its religious, political and literary context varies. Let us begin by reconstructing the historical situation in the land about 800 BCE, and then demonstrate how the definition of the genre fable illuminates the story. After closely examining the story-tellers' art in narrating this rather amazing tale of the King of Israel plundering the temple of Jerusalem, I shall conclude with the political and religious significance of the fable in the two versions of the story.

The period between the prophets Elijah and Amos (about 845-745 BCE) is not very well known to historians of Israel. Assyriologists can chronicle for us the rise of Assyrian power from c. 900 to 745, when Assyria begins breathing heavily down Israel's back. However, for the century before the appearance of the writing prophets, Amos,

Hosea, Isaiah and Micah, the Bible has just a few chapters in Kings and Chronicles (2 Kgs 11–15; 2 Chr 23–26). From them we learn of northern Israel's battles with Syria, southern Judah's battles with Edom, and the confrontation of north and south at the battle of Beth Shemesh between King Jehoash of Israel and King Amaziah of Judah, perhaps about 790.

The historian Siegfried Herrmann offers these approximate dates for the kings mentioned in the story above:

Israel	Judah
Jehu 842/41–815/14	Ahaziah 843/42–842/41
Jehoahaz 815/14–799-98	Joash [Jehoash] 836/35–797/96
Joash [Jehoash] 799/98–784/83	Amaziah 797/96–769/68

He notes that Jehoash of Israel is mentioned as a tributary of Adadnirari III (809-782) on an Assyrian stele.[1] From another archaeological find, the Samaria ostraca, probably contemporaneous with this one although there is no mention of a specific king on them, we learn that the economic power of kings in Israel had increased considerably since the tenth century.[2]

According to the Biblical authors, by the first part of the eighth century the principle of dynastic kingship with YHWH's approval is firmly fixed in both the north and the south (2 Kgs 10.30; 2 Sam 7),[3] but neither northern nor southern kings were strict Yahwists. The political and religious issues at stake had changed considerably since the time of the Judges (1200-1050) when Jotham uttered a political fable against Shechem's king, his brother Abimelech (Jdg 9). In this earlier fable of the trees trying to anoint a king over them, the very institution of kingship is satirized by their choosing a mean buckthorn to rule them, and the dynastic principle is still inferior to YHWH's charismatic choice of leaders.[4] By 800 the institution of hereditary kingship is no longer challenged, and the fable is delivered by royal messenger, instead of being declared in public to a group of people, as in Jotham's time. However, both fables do employ the same plant, the cedar of Lebanon, as a powerful symbol for kingship, and both of these plant stories function in the political realm to challenge power. Let us look more closely at Jehoash's fable now, with the definition of the genre in mind.

Jehoash's fable is a short, unreal story, featuring two talking plants, a thistle and a cedar, implicitly making the point that someone who is not strong should not fancy himself as more powerful than his superior. It is clearly a political fable. It was delivered by royal messenger, probably in both oral and written form to a king. The fable replies to a challenge to war and was presumably delivered in the Judean court. The purpose of the fable was not to incite anger directly, but to convince an opponent to desist from a planned course of action, out of a realistic appraisal of his own strength. Notice that Jehoash does not really directly identify himself with either the cedar or the beast, nor does he pitch north against south, but rather keeps the whole scene in the north. Nor does he threaten war, but warns of the inevitability of defeat if Amaziah persists. The thistle is portrayed as a naive country-bumpkin, who does not realize how small he really is.

As far as style is concerned, the repetition of the phrase 'which is in Lebanon' gives a poetic quality to the fable, as well as setting up the beat of the climax in the last line. The message within the fable, which itself is a message, is an entertaining irony. The content of that message, a bid for political power through marriage, is probably calculated to suggest to Amaziah that he really does not want war anyway. As noted in the previous chapter, the use of the beast at the end of the fable, a more realistic and naturalistic turn, signals the style of a court society with a central head.

Now that the basic characteristics of Jehoash's fable have been described, let us turn to examine more closely the broader literary context, so that the narrator's art can be appreciated more fully. For the storyteller's voice coincides with Jehoash's for only a brief moment, and since we cannot hear the author's tone or see the person's face, we must look outside the fable for clues.

The problem of motivation for the quarrel between the kings in the first place has been noted by several commentators who insist on reconstructing only pragmatic historical reasons to answer the questions of truth.[5] A careful reading of each version of the story provides motivation, but raises deeper political and religious questions.

Politically the northerners are ready and looking for a fight, to avenge what the Syrians have done to them (2 Kgs 12.18–13.5). Just as the Syrian king had trampled them into the dust (12.7), they will trample the Israelites (14.9). Just as the Syrians have taken booty from the temple (12.19) so also they take booty from the temple (14.14). In the south Amaziah has reason to think that God is not on the side of the Ephraimites (2 Chr 25.7), and that like his predecessors David and Solomon who have brought Edom under control, he too should now reunite the kingdom (2 Kgs 14.7; 2 Chr 25.11). The insight into the northern motivation comes primarily from the Kings story, the insight into the south comes from the Chronicles story. The fable itself deals with the problem of the political motivation, as noted above, as Jehoash attempts to persuade Amaziah that he really does not want a war. But further, a sober realism about power politics, regardless of motivation when viewed from another level, is symbolized by the beast. If a tiny nation seeks a political alliance with a larger one, are they not doomed to failure? The beast here is Jehoash; later it is Assyria, then Babylonia. The further irony lies in the religious fact that the people Israel, though very small in numbers and often vulnerable, does have an alliance—a covenant, sealed with a marriage formula, between itself and their true king. We shall explore this symbolism further below.

Thus far, the cultural level of truth on which these matters ring true is that of (a) continuity between art and culture, in regard to past events and customs, or (b) discontinuity between art and culture— the image of a strong northern Israel, when the writers and the audience know of its destruction by the Assyrians in 722. The fable is primarily a moral genre, however, and so it offers (c) ideas about what a good culture might be. Johoash is telling Amaziah to be realistic about his power position, and never to enter war solely for political gain. But how are we supposed to feel towards these kings, and further, how are we to judge their actions? The fable fails to restrain Amaziah, and the ensuing battle results in the capture of the Judean king, the plundering of the temple and the palace, the destruction of a good portion of the northern wall of Jerusalem, and the taking of hostages—all by northern Israel! Yet this episode is never used in an indictment of the north by subsequent writers, and has virtually been passed over in silence. How is the audience to evaluate these events?

There are four political and religious issues raised in the immediate literary context of the fable which help the audience know how they are to evaluate the kings and their actions: (i) the principle of individual retribution (2 Kgs 14.6); (ii) the necessity of inquiring of only YHWH for directions (2 Chr 25.15ff.); (iii) the subordination of even a Davidic king, the temple of Jerusalem, the city, and its people to God's covenant; and (iv) the violation of divine sovereignty by the pretensions to power of human kings. The first is raised most sharply in the Kings story, the second in the Chronicles story. The fable itself illustrates these last two issues in subtle irony with the cedar of Lebanon. Each king is evaluated individually, and rather even-handedly by our two storytellers. Both do correct things; both make mistakes. The principle for this evaluation is in the story of Amaziah, who is said to follow one of the commandments, 'Each one should be punished only for his own sin' (Deut 24.16; 2 Kgs 14.6; 2 Chr 25.4b). The prophets Jeremiah and Ezekiel also reflected on the broader implications of this commandment in dealing with the problem of suffering during the Babylonian nightmare (Jer 31.27-30; Ezek 18). I am suggesting that the author of Kings in particular, who treats all the northern and southern kings, was trying his best not to criticize either Jehoash or Amaziah simply on the basis of mistakes made by rulers before them, like Jeroboam I or Athaliah, but rather to look at each one's actions in his own lifetime. We the audience are also not allowed a smug dismissal of these kings, but are encouraged to look at each one individually.

The second religious and political issue raised by the surrounding story is the necessity of inquiring of only YHWH for direction. While a subtheme in the Kings story (Jehoash's inquiry of Elisha [2 Kgs 13.14-19]), it is a major theme in the Chronicles story of Jehoash and Amaziah and provides the central motivation for all that happens (2 Chr 25.14-28). Because Amaziah inquired of the deity he captured from the Edomites when he should have known better, he is defeated; Judah falls; and Jerusalem is overcome. So simple an explanation as the kings' and peoples' plurality of worship, which is usually employed by the Kings author to explain or to judge events, does not suffice to account for the humiliation of Judah by Israel. A more serious violation of correct action is the consultation of other deities instead of YHWH's prophets. Thus in the Chronicles story Amaziah is in trouble from the very first message he sends, and Jehoash is acting with divine approval (note the echo of the Holy War formula, 'that they might be delivered by hand . . . ', 2 Chr 25.20). The audience is being warned to consult the true prophet from God at every major juncture. For Amaziah was told at first that God was not with the Ephraimites at the time of the Edomite battle (v. 7), but then he did not consult correctly before the battle with Ephraim and found that God was on their side! Amaziah forgot the words of the prophet, 'It is God who has the power to reinforce or to defeat' (v. 8).

The third religious issue raised by the story of Jehoash's fable is treated with great restraint—the subordination of even a Davidic descendant, the temple, the wall and the people of Jerusalem to God's purpose and covenant. This issue, as well as the fourth one, the violation of divine sovereignty by the pretensions to power of human kings, is suggested by the lofty image of the cedar of Lebanon in the fable. We the audience, and undoubtedly the first audience of Kings and Chronicles, know of the disaster of 587, when an even more devastating sack of Jerusalem and Judah occurred. Yet rather than passing over the event of 790 in total silence as too painful, an author records it, and makes sense of it. Of course it is well known to readers of Kings and Chronicles that the authors' judgment on the event of 587, that the people and rulers were not strict enough Yahwists, is stated explicitly several times in these works. In 2 Kgs 14 and 2 Chr 25, however, the same point is more subtly made in the fable of Jehoash by means of the symbolism of the cedar of Lebanon. The cedar rises above the dealings of human kings, beasts and thistles as they are. There is no need for a chosen son or daughter to solidify the basic arrangement (a human ruler as intermediary between God and the people). It has been there all along since Sinai.

A thorough literary study of Jehoash's fable would require: first, defining the literary unity surrounding the fable, delineating its structures, and noting key words. The second set of questions would concern the oral and literary sources and traditions employed by the storytellers, their identities and their audiences' identities. The third set of questions would concern the needs of their audiences, and how they shaped their stories to answer these needs, being true to their own creative impulse for shaping society and religious experience. While suggesting answers to these questions above, a detailed study lies beyond the purpose of this chapter.[6]

Genre studies are part of a larger process, particularly valuable in understanding cultures other than one's own. It is hoped that this genre analysis of Jehoash's thistle fable has set forth the conventional and the creative adaptation of the form to a particular situation, that it has shown how a fictional genre could ring true, and that it has also laid bare the broader political and religious perspectives from which we are meant to view the fable, from both below the beast, and above the cedar.

NOTES

Notes to Chapter 1

SAGA

1. Burke O. Long, 'II Kings 3: An Oracular Fulfillment Narrative', *Seminar Papers* (The Society of Biblical Literature, 1971), 183-205.
2. 'Legend: A Case Study in OT Formcritical Terminology', *CBQ* 34 (1972), 166. Reprinted as Chapter 3 of this volume.
3. 'Arten der Erzählung in der Genesis', *Forschung am alten Testament* (Munich: Kaiser, 1964), 31.
4. *Abraham in History and Tradition* (New Haven: Yale University Press, 1975), 131-138.
5. *Form Criticism of the Old Testament* (Philadelphia: Fortress, 1971), 350.
6. I have maintained the use of two separate terms. *Sage* may imply a narrative form which does not have in mind the Icelandic literature, which we shall distinguish by the term saga.
7. 'Volkstümliche, altüberlieferte, poetische Erzählung, die Personen oder Ergnisse der Vergangenheit behandelt' (*Genesis* [Göttingen: Vandenhoeck und Ruprecht, ⁶1964], viii).
8. Gunkel, *Genesis*, viii. 'Ein Hauptkennzeichen ist, dass die Sage ursprünglich als mündliche Überlieferung...'
9. Gunkel, *Genesis*, ix. 'Die Sage... redet über die Dinge, die dem Volke am Herzen liegen, über das Persönliche und Private...'
10. Gunkel, *Genesis*, ix. 'Anders aber bei der Sage, die nur z.t. aus Überlieferung, z.T. aber aus der Phantasie schöpft. Bei der Schöpfung ist kein Mensch zugegen gewesen; keine menschliche Überlieferung reicht in die Zeit der Entstehung unseres Geschlechtes, der Urvölker, der Ursprachen.'
11. Gunkel, *Genesis*, 10. 'Das deutlichtste Kennzeichen der Sage ist, dass sie nicht selten Dinge berichtet, die uns unglaubwürdig sind.'
12. Gunkel, *Genesis*, 12. 'Die Sage aber ist ihrer Natur nach Poesie: sie will erfreuen, erheben, begeistern, rühren.'
13. Tucker, *Form Criticism*, 30, and Werner Klatt, *Hermann Gunkel* (*FRLANT*, 100; Göttingen: Vandenhoeck und Ruprecht, 1969), 126f.
14. Gunkel, vii.
15. André Jolles, *Einfache Formen* (Darmstadt: Niemeyer, ²1958), 63.
16. Gunkel, *Genesis*, xii-xiii.

17. *Traditionsgeschichtliche Untersuchungen zum Richterbuch* (BBB, 18; Bonn: Hanstein, 1966), 346. 'Nun beginnt Gunkel, wenn auch noch behutsam, mit einer Wertung der Gattung vom Standpunkt des Historikers aus, ohne andere Standpunkt zu berücksichtigen, indem er die Erzählungsgattungen in zwei Gruppen einteilet . . . '
18. *Anatomy of Criticism: Four Essays* (Princeton: University Press, 1957), 246f.
19. Cited from Klatt, 128. '1. Einen bestimmter Schatz von *Gedanken und Stimmungen*, 2. eine deutliche *Formensprache*, in der diese sich äussern, 3. einen *Sitz im Leben*, aus dem Inhalt und Form erst verstanden werden können.'
20. Klatt.
21. Jolles, 67.
22. Jolles.
23. Jolles, 68.
24. Jolles, 72.
25. Jolles.
26. Jolles.
27. Jolles, 75.
28. Jolles, 82.
29. Jolles, 87f.
30. Westermann, 'Arten der Erzählung in der Genesis'.
31. Westermann, 39 n. 23.
32. Westermann, 38.
33. Stefan Einarsson, *A History of Icelandic Literature* (New York: Johns Hopkins Press, 1957), 122.
34. *The Nature of Narrative* (Oxford: University Press, 1966), 50.
35. Einarsson, 122ff.
36. Einarsson, 126.
37. Einarsson, 128f.
38. Einarsson.
39. *Myth and Religion of the North: The Religion of Ancient Scandinavia* (Chicago: Holt, Rinehart and Winston, 1964), 17ff.
40. 'Saga', *Encyclopedia Britannica* 19 (1972), 812.
41. Scholes and Kellogg, 50.
42. Scholes and Kellogg.
43. *Epic and Romance; Essays on Medieval Literature* (New York: Dover, 1957), 186.
44. Ker, 213f.
45. Einarsson, 133.
46. Einarsson, 133f.
47. *Legends of Genesis* (new edn; New York: Schocken, 1964), 42.
48. Gunkel, *Legends*, 42ff.
49. Gunkel, *Legends*, 45f.

50. Gunkel, *Legends*, 186.

51. For a full discussion, see my article, 'The Annunciation in the Birth Narrative of Ishmael', *BR* 17 (1972), 1.

52. Neff, 9f.

53. G. von Rad, *Genesis* (Philadelphia: Westminster, 1972), 197.

54. E.A. Speiser, *Genesis* (New York: Doubleday, 1964), 127.

55. The healing narratives of Epidauros begin with the identification of the woman who is visited by Asklepios.

56. *Nātattî* (Gen 17.8, 20, etc.).

57. For a discussion of the idiom, *kā'ēt ḥayyâ*, see n. 82 below.

58. C. Bonner, 'Traces of Thaumaturgic Technique in the Miracles', *HTR* 20 (1927), 171f., where loud cries, roarings, or bellowings are described as part of a healing technique used in curing disease.

59. J. Behm, *Die Handauflegung im Urchristentum* (Leipzig: A. Deichert, 1911), 192ff. For the healing touch of the king, cf. J. Gray, 'Canaanite Kingship in Theory and Practice', *VT* 2 (1952), 207ff.

60. Naaman expects Elisha to invoke the name of the deity (2 Kgs 5.11). Cf. P.W. Fiebig, *Jüdische Wundergeschichten des neutestamentlichen Zeitalters unter besonderer Berücksichtigung ihres Verhältnisse zum Neuen Testament bearbeitet* (Tübingen: J.C.B. Mohr [Paul Siebeck], 1911), 35ff.

61. Is 38.21 and 2 Kgs 20.7.

62. Von Rad, *Genesis*, 202.

63. J. Skinner, *Genesis* (ICC; Edinburgh: T. and T. Clark, 1930), 301f.

64. G. Quell, 'Das Phänomen des Wunders im Alten Testament', *Verbannung und Heimkehr* (Tübingen: J.C.B. Mohr [Paul Siebeck], 1961), 264ff.

65. Speiser, *Genesis*, 125.

66. Franz Delitzsch, *Neuer Commentar über die Genesis* (Leipzig: Dörffling und Franke, 1887), 38.

67. Otto Procksch, *Die Genesis* (Leipzig: A. Deichert, 1924), 522.

68. Von Rad, *Genesis*, 198.

69. Quell, 265f.

70. Then as now the relative age of senility is indeterminate. The diminution and loss of virility are well attested in the Old Testament (2 Sam 19.35f. and Eccl 12.3ff.). King David loses sexual potency in his later years (1 Kgs 1.4). Even the gods became senile; cf. M. Pope, *El in the Ugaritic Texts* (Leiden: E.J. Brill, 1955), 39ff. There are, of course, notable exceptions. Moses retains his virility until his death at age one hundred and twenty (Deut 34.7). Cf. W.F. Albright, 'The "Natural Force" of Moses in the Light of Ugaritic', *BASOR* 94 (1944), 32ff. E. Otto, *Die biographischen Inschriften der ägyptischen Spätzeit* (Leiden: E.J. Brill, 1954), 136, describes an inscription which recounts that a man of ninety-six retained his sexual vigor.

71. R. Bultmann, *The History of the Synoptic Tradition* (New York: Harper and Row, 1963), 221.

72. 2 Kgs 4.16.

73. 2 Kgs 5.11.

74. O. Weinreich, *Antike Heilungswunder* (Giessen: A. Töpelmann, 1909), 87f.

75. One must ask whether the word *yiṣḥāq* is a later intrusion into the story. Although the above observations make most probable the disbelief of Sarah and Abraham in the word of healing which comes to them, the expression of that unbelief by the verb *ṣḥq* is questionable since the semantic field of the word is bounded by the meanings of rejoice and play (BDB, 850). In Gen 19.15 and Jdg 16.25, the usage points toward jest; the notion of derision is most apparent in Ezek 23.32 where it is used in parallelism with *l'g*. The use of laughter or doubt occurs irrespective of its reference to Isaac in these narratives. Whether the word used to express this motif was *ṣḥq* cannot finally be answered. Cf. Martin Noth, *A History of Pentateuchal Traditions* (Englewood Cliffs: Prentice-Hall, 1972) 107-108, where the relation of Isaac to Abraham is taken as a secondary development in the history of tradition.

76. The word *pele'*, contained in the response of Yahweh to Sarah, is a technical term for wonder. Its presence in a healing narrative is unusual, but not out of character since it reflects the power of Yahweh. For the use of the term, cf. W. Vollborn, 'Wunder', *RGG³*, VI, 1834f.; Quell, 294ff.

77. Robert M. Grant, *Miracle and Natural Law in Graeco-Roman and Early Christian Thought* (Amsterdam: North Holland, 1952), 154. Cf. Lk 18.27.

78. In 1 Kgs 14 a woman, the wife of the king, wearing a disguise comes to a prophet. Before she enters the room where the prophet awaits her, he declares not only who she is but also what her petition is. The prophet's announcement demonstrates his power. A sign may accompany the word addressed to an individual as an indication of the pronouncement's divine origin, e.g., Is 38 and 2 Kgs 20.

79. The infinitive absolute *šōb* in v. 10 denotes the certainty of Yahweh's return, while *lammō'ēd* in v. 14 sets an appointed time for his visitation. The two clauses are co-ordinated by *wᵉhinnēh* in v. 10 but *wᵉ* in v. 14. *ben* precedes *lᵉśārâ* in v. 10 but follows *lᵉśārâ* in v. 14.

80. A constant temporal construction where concomitant events are described (GKC, 501).

81. There is no indication that Sarah conceived at the moment the promise was given or that she gave birth on the exact day of Yahweh's return. Therefore, it is extremely dubious that this passage may be used to assert that Israel possessed a notion of a twelve-month pregnancy. Cf. David Daube, *Studies in Biblical Law* (New York: KTAV, 1969), 148 n. 6: 'As for the Hittite Code's contemplating a pregnancy of ten months it is interesting to note the XII Tables do the same (iv. 4). Gellius says (Noctes Atticae 3, 16.1) that *multa opinio est, eaque iam pro vero recepta ... gigni hominem septimo, rarentur, numquam octavo, saepa nono, saepius numero decimo*

mense. Ancient medicine was not very clear about the problem, as is evident from the chapter in Gellius from which I have just quoted . . . Where a child is promised by God or a prophet in the Old Testament, the birth seems always to take place a year after the promise (Genesis xvii.21, xviii.10, 14, I Samuel i.20, II Kings iv. 16f.' However, the Sumerians were aware of a nine-month gestation period; cf. S.N. Kramer, *From the Tablets of Sumer* (Indian Hills: Falcon's Wing Press, 1956), 173: 'One day being her one month, two days being her two months, nine days being her nine months, the months of "womanhood"'. Also 2 Macc 7.27.

82. For a discussion of the meaning of the idiom, *kā'ēt ḥayyâ*, cf. O. Loretz, *'K't ḥyh* wie jetz ums Jahr Gen 18,10', *Biblica* 43 (1962), 75ff. Akkadian *balatu* (life) may mean 'the coming year' (*The Assyrian Dictionary of the Oriental Institute of the University of Chicago*, II, [Chicago, 1965], 51f.). Texts from the Judean desert dating from the first and second centuries AD set the time for the renewal of contrast by the phrase, *kdy hy'* (J.T. Milik, 'Deux documents inedits du Désert de Juda', *Biblica* 38 (1957), 256; cf. Reuven Yaron, 'Note on a Judean Deed of Sale of Field', *BASOR* 150 (1958), 28: 'I wish to suggest that *kdy hy'* does not mean "while (I am) alive [Milik's translation]," but "in a year's time." It is equivalent to the Biblical *ka'ēt ḥayyâ* . . . This is supported by the fact that the Egyptian *aneaōsis* clause usually refers to the renewal of the document one year after it was issued.'

83. In the prophetic legends the prophet often foretells an occurrence with precision. A prominent feature is the prediction of an event within an allotted period of time:

> This year you shall die (Jer 28.16).
> On the third day you shall go up to the house of the Lord (2 Kgs 20.5).
> When your feet come to the city, the boy will die (1 Kgs 14.12).

Within these three examples there is a wide variety of formulation: a nominal clause, a verbal clause, and co-ordinate clauses. Yet each declare the time when an event is to occur. S. Mowinckel, *Prophecy and Tradition: The Prophetic Books in the Light of the Study of the Growth and History of the Tradition* (Oslo: J. Dybwad, 1946), 45: ' . . . prophet narratives where we are confronted with a concrete situation and hear the message that the prophet announced exactly then and there. The narratives of Eliah [*sic*] and Elisha, and other prophetic legends in 1 and 2 Samuel; the Isaiah legends in Kings and Is 36—39; Baruch's narratives about Jeremish in Jer 26—45 . . . ' Cf. also A. Jepsen, *Nabi: Soziologische Studien zur alttestamentlichen Literatur und Religionsgeschichte* (München: C.H. Beck, 1934), 130.

84. The exact source division of Gen 21.1-2 is complex, but most commentators assign 21.2b to P. For the stylistic similarities of 17.21b and 21.2b, cf. Paul Humbert, 'Die literarische Zweiheit des Priester-Codex in der Genesis', *ZAW* 58 (1940-41), 51.

85. Gunkel, *Genesis*, 199.

86. Quell, *op. cit.*, 278.

87. To call these stories family narratives is an unfortunate designation, since it seeks to classify them according to their setting, i.e. the home (cf. Westermann, *op. cit.*, 61). This would mean that a number of miracle stories could be so classified, for one of their characteristics is that the miracle is done away from the public eye, in the home of a prophet or individual (1 Kgs 14; 2 Kgs 4; etc.), but very seldom before the public at large. Nature miracles by contrast are publicly demonstrated as in 1 Kgs 18.

88. For the gift for fertility, Hos 11.8 represents a striking example; cf. James Pritchard, 'Motifs of Old Testament Miracles', *CQ* 27 (1950), 106.

89. Mary Hamilton, *Incubation or the Cure of Disease in Pagan Temples and Christian Churches* (London, 1906), 8, text 2.

90. Emma and Ludwig Edelstein, 'Asclepius', *A Collection and Interpretation of the Testimonies* (Publications of the Institute of the History of Medicine, 2nd series, Vol. II; Baltimore, 1945), 187.

Notes to Chapter 2

THE MOSES NARRATIVES AS HEROIC SAGA

1. Martin Buber, *Moses. The Revelation and the Covenant* (New York: Harper, 1946), 200. See also Ann Margaret Vater, *The Communication of Messages and Oracles as a Narration Medium in the Old Testament* (Dissertation, Yale, 1976); Maurice Luker, *The Figure of Moses in the Plague Traditions* (Dissertation, Drew, 1968).

2. Brevard S. Childs, *Exodus. A Critical, Theological Commentary* (OTL; Philadelphia: Westminster, 1974), 351-60. See also James Muilenburg, 'The Intercession of the Covenant Mediator (Exodus 33.1a, 12-17)', in *Words and Meanings. Essays Presented to David Winton Thomas* (ed. Peter R. Ackroyd, Barnabas Lindars; Cambridge: University Press, 1968), 159-81.

3. Klaus Koch, 'Der Tod des Religionsstifters. Erwägungen über aas Verhältnis Israels zur Geschichte der altorientalischen Religionen', *KuD* 8 (1962), 100-23; F. Baumgärtel, 'Der Tod des Religionsstifter', *KuD* 9 (1963), 223-33; Rolf Rendtorff, 'Mose als Religionsstifter? Ein Beitrag zur Diskussion über die Anfänge der israelitischen Religion', in *Gesammelte Studien zum Alten Testament* (Theologische Bücherei, 57; München: Kaiser, 1975), 152-71. There are still other categories. See the review by Vater, 122-35.

4. Martin Noth, *A History of Pentateuchal Traditions* (tr. Bernhard W. Anderson; Englewood Cliffs: Prentice-Hall, 1972), 156.

5. Dewey M. Beegle, *Moses, the Servant of Yahweh* (Grand Rapids: Eerdmans, 1972), 15-30.

6. A quasi-historical question could be posed here. What office does the literature depict for the figure of Moses?

7. Noth, 156.

8. Noth, 170-75.

9. George W. Coats, 'Legendary Motifs in the Moses Death Reports', *CBQ* 39 (1977), 34-44.

10. Vater, 138-139.

11. Noth, 161.

12. It should be noted here that the logical consequence of the hypothesis is not to undermine the thesis that there are different themes, as Noth suggested. It is to undermine the assumption that the different themes are independent.

13. See Childs, 8-11.

14. Bernhard W. Anderson, *Understanding the Old Testament* (3rd edn; Englewood Cliffs: Prentice-Hall, 1975), 48.

15. Joseph Campbell, *The Hero with a Thousand Faces* (Bollingen Series, 17; Princeton: University Press, 1949), 30.

16. Anderson, 48.

17. John van Seters, *Abraham in History and Tradition* (New Haven: Yale University Press, 1975), 131-37. See particularly 131 n. 19. I would agree completely with his objections to current translations of the German term *Sage*. I would include in the objections his own term. Legend can be simply something read or spoken, thus *Sage*. But it can also have a more precise generic meaning. See Ron Hals, 'Legend: A Case Study in Old Testament Form-Critical Terminology', *CBQ* 34 (1972), 166-76 (reprinted as Chapter 3 of this volume). If objections against using legend for this kind of narrative nonetheless arise, then some other term must be proposed, for Hals and others have correctly distinguished a genre of narrative material. I would think that until a more workable term acceptable to a larger range of scholars in the field appears, legend should be reserved for the genre Hals defines. *Sage* might then be represented with a more neutral term such as narrative or story, or perhaps the more technical term 'tale'. On 'saga' see Neff, Chapter 1.

18. Klaus Baltzer, *Die Biographie der Propheten* (Neukirchen-Vluyn: Neukirchener Verlag, 1975), 38-53.

19. Sylvan Barnet, Morton Berman, William Burto, *A Dictionary of Literary, Dramatic, and Cinematic Terms* (Boston: Little, Brown, and Co., 1971), 11.

20. Barnett, Berman, Burto, 11.

21. Coats, 'Legendary Motifs', 34-44.

22. See Brevard S. Childs, 'The Birth of Moses', *JBL* 84 (1965), 109-22.

23. George W. Coats, 'Moses in Midian', *JBL* 92 (1973), 3-10.

24. George W. Coats, 'Moses Versus Amalek: Aetiology and Legend in

Exod xvii 8-16', in *Congress Volume Edinburgh* (VTSup, 2; Leiden, Brill, 1975), 29-41.

25. George W. Coats, 'Humility and Honor: A Moses Legend in Numbers 12', *Art and Meaning: Rhetoric in Biblical Literature* (JSOTS, 19; ed. D.J.A. Clines, D.M. Gunn, and A.J. Hauser; Sheffield: JSOT Press, 1982), 97-107.

26. Aelred Cody, 'Exodus 18,12: Jethro Accepts a Covenant with the Israelites', *Bib* 49 (1968), 153-66.

27. Norman Habel, 'The Form and Significance of the Call Narratives', *ZAW* 77 (1965), 297-323.

28. Campbell, 69-77.

29. Childs, 56-61. Childs argues against this proposal as developed by Seebass, for example, on the basis of (i) a syntactical problem in the verse. The announcement of worship on the mountain is connected with the reference to a sign asyndetically. It thus has more to do with the sign than the preceding promise. My suggestion does not deny the importance of the phrase, however. It suggests that the announcement appears as a result of the sign. (ii) The stereotype in the promise for presence could hardly serve as a sign. My suggestion, however, is that the sign lies in the play on the name, not simply in the promise. The sign is in effect the name. This suggestion would have some advantage over the one offered by Childs. It does not require an explanation that the description of the sign has been displaced. To the contrary, it can look forward to vv. 13-15, the *idem per idem* formula, and finally the gift of the name. It is the name that confirms Moses' commission, the authority of both the sender and the sent.

30. Coats, 'Aetiology and Legend', 35. The point here does not deny that the power symbolized by the rod comes from God. See Childs, 79. But it does suggest that Moses is not simply vehicle. Moses is to do something.

31. Childs, 52.

32. George W. Coats, 'Despoiling the Egyptians', *VT* 18 (1968), 450-57.

33. H. Gross, 'Der Glaube an Mose nach Exodus (4.14, 19), in *Wort— Gebot—Glaube: Beiträge zur Theologie des Alten Testaments* (ed. H.J. Stoebe, J.J. Stamm, E. Jenni; ATANT, 59; Zürich: Zwingli, 1970), 57-66.

34. Childs, 54.

35. Childs, 55.

36. Childs, 56.

37. Childs, 356.

38. George W. Coats, 'The King's Loyal Opposition: Obedience and Authority in Exodus 32—34', in *Canon and Authority. Essays in Old Testament Religion and Theology* (ed. George W. Coats, Burke O. Long; Philadelphia: Fortress, 1977), 91-109.

Notes to Chapter 3

LEGEND

*Reprinted by permission from *CBQ* 34 (1972), 166-76.
1. *RGG* 5 (1913), 174-98.
2. G. Fohrer, *Introduction to the Old Testament* (tr. D. Green; Nashville: Abingdon, 1968), 90-93. H. Wildberger, 'Sage und Legende', *Biblisch-Historisches Handwörterbuch* (ed. B. Reicke & L. Rost; Göttingen: Vandenhoeck & Ruprecht, 1966), III, 1641: E. Jacob, 'Sagen und Legenden', *RGG*, V (1961), 1302; and A. Weiser, *The Old Testament: Its Formation and Development* (tr. D. Barton; New York: Association, 1961), 61, follow a similar practice.
3. Fohrer, *Introduction*, 86.
4. O. Eissfeldt, *The Old Testament: an Introduction* (tr. P.R. Ackroyd; New York: Harper & Row, 1965), 34.
5. A. Bentzen, *Introduction to the Old Testament* (Copenhagen: Gads, 1948), I, 234.
6. Bentzen, *ibid.*
7. *RGG*, V (1913), 194-96.
8. Cf. W. Klatt, *Hermann Gunkel* (FRLANT, 100; Göttingen: Vandenhoeck & Ruprecht, 1969), 175.
9. *RGG*, V (1913), 178-79.
10. *HKAT* 3,1 (1902), xi-lxxxix. The first edition is not available to me.
11. H. Gunkel, *Legends of Genesis* (tr. W. Carruth; Chicago: Open Court, 1901).
12. B.W. Anderson, *Understanding the Old Testament* (2nd edn; Englewood Cliffs, New Jersey: Prentice-Hall, 1966), 164.
13. H. Gunkel, *Legends of Genesis* (new edn; New York: Schocken, 1964), xi-xii.
14. Anderson, *Understanding*, 584.
15. Bentzen, *Introduction*, I, 233.
16. The use of Danish *sagn* by Bentzen and Norwegian *sagn* by S. Mowinckel, 'Legend', *IDB*, III (1962), 108-109, seems unlikely to catch on, which is probably just as well in view of the potential additional confusion.
17. Bentzen, *loc. cit.*
18. K. Koch, *The Growth of the Biblical Tradition* (tr. S. Cupitt; New York: Scribners, 1969), 195.
19. A. Jolles, *Einfache Formen* (2nd edn; Tübingen: Niemeyer, 1958), 23-61.
20. While all readings on a particular occasion are likely to have the same or at least a related *Sitz im Leben*, the current practice in worship services reveals clearly that a similar *Sitz* does not guarantee a similar *Gattung*.

21. Cf. G. von Rad, *Genesis* (tr. J. Marks; Philadelphia: Westminster, 1961), 31, and Koch, *Growth*, 151-53.
22. D. Haring, 'Legend', *Encyclopedia Americana* 17 (1962), 214.
23. Haring, *ibid.*
24. Haring, *ibid.*
25. Haring, *ibid.*
26. So Bentzen, *Introduction*, 240; Eissfeldt, *The Old Testament: an Introduction*, 46; Fohrer, *Introduction*, 92; and Weiser, *The Old Testament: Its Formation*, 62.
27. S. Mowinckel, 'Legend', *IDB*, III (1962), 108-109.
28. Mowinckel, *op. cit.*, 109.
29. Koch, *Growth*, 184-205.
30. Cf. G. von Rad, *Old Testament Theology* (tr. D. Stalker; Edinburgh: Oliver and Boyd, 1965), II, 34-35.
31. K. Koch, *Growth*, 198.
32. Koch, *op. cit.*, 202.
33. Von Rad, *Old Testament Theology*, II, 207-208.
34. Koch, *Growth*, 204.
35. O. Plöger, *Die Prophetengeschichten der Samuel- und Königsbücher* (Dissertation, Greifswald, 1937). This work is not available to me.

Notes to Chapter 4

BALAAM

*Reprinted by permission from *BR* 18 (1973), 21-29.
1. Martin Noth, *Numbers, a Commentary* (tr. James D. Martin; Philadelphia: Westminster, 1968), 171-72, 178.
2. Hugo Gressmann, *Die Schriften des Alten Testaments*, (2nd edn; Göttingen: Vandenhoeck & Ruprecht, 1920), I, 120-21. Cf. also Sigmund Mowinckel, 'Der Ursprung der Bileamsage', *ZAW* 70 (1930), 233-71.
3. Cf. esp. James A. Wharton, 'The Command to Bless; an Exposition of Numbers 22.41–23.25', *Interp* 13 (1959), 37-48.
4. Martin Noth, *A History of Pentateuchal Traditions* (tr. Bernhard W. Anderson; Englewood Cliffs: Prentice-Hall, 1972), 78.
5. Mowinckel, 238, comments on this problem: 'Bemerkenswert ist, dass der Anschlag Bālāks misslingt, und schiedlich-friedlich gehen Israel und Mo'ab auseinander, man möchte sagen; auf Nimmerwiederschen: kein Krieg zwischen ihnen, kein Resultat'. H. Gressmann, *Mose und Seine Zeit, ein Kommentar zu den Mose-Sagen* (FRLANT, 18; Göttingen, Vandenhoeck and Ruprecht, 1913), 322, also comments on the problem. But cf. Mowinckel's critique.
6. On the conclusion of the story, cf. below, n. 11.

7. Noth, *Numbers*, 171, 175, sees this repetition as a doublet and uses it as evidence for splitting the verse, as well as the story as a whole, into two parallel accounts. I cannot believe, however, that such repetitions must necessarily indicate two sources. Cf. the comment below, n. 9.

8. W.F. Albright, 'The Oracles of Balaam', *JBL* 63 (1944), 233, concludes that Balaam must have become 'a convert to Yahwism, and that he later abandoned Israel and joined the Midianites in fighting against the Yahwists (Num 31.8, 16)'. But we must be careful not to make a simple equation between diverse stages in the history of the Balaam tradition and a biographical sketch harmonizing all of the diversity into a single layer. Cf. Wharton's comments, p. 41 n. 10.

9. Gerhard von Rad, *Moses* (World Christian Books, 32; New York: Association, 1959), 73, concludes that 'Balaam still intends to curse the people and makes all the necessary preparations for doing so'. But it seems important to me that the story never commits Balaam's action to either blessing or curse. He does nothing but obey the word Yahweh puts into his mouth.

10. Nor does it mean a shift from one source to another. Noth, *Numbers*, 171, argues: 'From the point of view of content the two self-contained sections, 22.41–23.26 and 23.28–24.19, present obvious doublets, the former with two "Balaam discourses", forms the main part of the E-version, while the latter again with two "Balaam discourses", forms the main part of the J-version'. Cf. also O. Eissfeldt, 'Die Komposition der Bileam-Erzählung. Eine Nachprüfung von Rudolphs Beitrag zur Hexateuchkritik', *ZAW* 57 (1939), 212-41. Sources may lie behind this story. But if they do, they cannot account for the structural unity provided by the dominant motif. Cf. Noth's difficulty in separating the sources in 22.2-40 (*Numbers*, 171). One would be forced to conclude that R is more creative than either J or E.

11. The conclusion of the story appears, it seems to me, in 24.14a, with Balaam's announcement of his departure. This final part of Balaam's speech may be complemented by the narrative conclusion in 24.25. The intervening material does not stand in an integral relationship with the narration down to 24.14. The unifying motif does not appear here. There is no reference to sacrifice, no blesing or curse on Israel. Following Balaam's announcement in v. 14a, this material functions only as an appendix.

12. For details in this definition of legend, cf. Ronald M. Hals, 'Legend: A Case Study in OT Form-Critical Terminology', *CBQ* 34 (1972), 166-76 (reprinted as Chapter 3 above). To recognize that the story is a legend keys the interpretation of the story by pointing to Balaam as the hero, not God or the Word of God. A parallel might help. In Gen 22, Abraham appears as the hero of a legend. The story demonstrates the virtue of his obedience to God's command. The command is not the hero. Not even God appears here as hero. Rather, the hero is clearly Abraham, with his unswerving devotion to

God. Cf. George W. Coats, 'Abraham's Sacrifice of Faith; A Form-Critical Study of Genesis 22', *Interp* 27 (1973), 389-400.
13. Noth, *History*, 76, refers to the story as a legend, both in a citation from Mowinckel, and in his own description. But the term reflects a problem in translation. Noth's original refers to the story as the 'Bileam-Balak-Erzählung', Mowinckel's as the 'Bileam Balak-Saga.' On the other hand, Mowinckel notes (pp. 260-62), that in the Elohist the saga has been reformulated as a legend, a characteristic of the Elohist. Mowinckel moves in the right direction here. His definition of legend, however, belabors the religious content of the story rather than the structural emphasis on a virtue as a model for edification of subsequent generations. Moreover, source critics should avoid the assumption that all such edifying legends derive by definition from the Elohist. Cf. Coats, 'Abraham's Sacrifice of Faith', 396 n. 7.
14. Wharton, 41.
15. Wharton, 41. The same point can be seen in the work of J. Lindblom, *Prophecy in Ancient Israel* (Philadelphia: Muhlenberg Press, 1962), 90-95. On p. 91 he observes: 'Balaam was *forced* [italics mine] to pronounce a blessing instead of the expected curse'. But the story shows no force moving Balaam out of his original intention.
16. Noth, *Numbers*, 175.
17. Noth, *Numbers*, 175.
18. Wharton, 45.
19. Von Rad, 74, concludes that 'Balaam has ceased to be master of himself. He behaves like an automaton.' It seems to me to be necessary to emphasize the opposite point. Balaam does not act contrary to his own will, or without will. He charts his own course and follows it to its conclusion. Cf. Coats, 'Abraham's Sacrifice of Faith', 398 n. 11. It would be helpful here to consider the contribution of other saints, particularly foreign saints, to Israel's theology. Cf. Ezek 14.20.

Notes to Chapter 5

TALE

1. Claus Westermann, 'Arten der Erzählung in der Genesis', in *Forschung am Alten Testament* (München: Kaiser, 1965), 9-91. The key term for Westermann is *der Spannungsbogen*, 'arc of tension'.
2. Use of the term 'exposition' should not be confused with the use of the same word to refer to a particular kind of commentary on a text. The fourth section of discussion about any Biblical book for the *Interpreter's Bible* carries the title: 'Exposition'. That kind of exposition also attempts to expose

the crucial elements in a pericope. But it does so from an interpretative stance *outside* of the pericope, an element that observes the whole and constructs comments about it. In the sense in which I use it, however, 'exposition' is a structural element of the tale, a part of the whole; it fulfills an intrinsic function for the whole. It provides information necessary for the following elements in the story to accomplish their functions.

3. See the comments on formulas for exposition in Wolfgang Richter, *Die sogenannten vorprophetischen Berufungsberichte. Eine literaturwissenschaftliche Studie zu 1. Sam 9,1-10, 16, Ex 3f. und Ri 6,11b-17* (FRLANT, 101; Göttingen: Vandenhoeck und Ruprecht, 1970), 30 and n. 3.

4. Axel Olrik, 'Epic Laws of Folk Narrative', in *The Study of Folklore* (ed. Alan Dundes; Englewood Cliffs: Prentice-Hall, 1965), 132. Olrik's term is the German noun *Sage*, preserved in the English translation in its German form. The term is obviously not a simple equivalent for 'saga'. See Chapter 1 in this volume on saga, by Robert W. Neff. The German term is imprecise, embracing more than one distinct genre. Yet, Olrik seems to have a genre with limited structure in view. Perhaps for Olrik, *Sage* is a story *told* in a folk setting, thus at least similar to tale as a story *told* in a folk setting.

5. Olrik, 134-35.

6. Sylvan Barnet, Morton Berman, and William Burto, *A Dictionary of Literary, Dramatic, and Cinematic Terms* (2nd edn; Boston: Little, Brown, and Company, 1971), 101.

7. Westermann, 11-34.

8. See the brief remarks toward this same conclusion in my commentary, *Genesis, with an Introduction to Narrative Literature* (FOTL, 1; Grand Rapids: Eerdmans, 1983), 7-8.

9. For details on this exegesis, see my forthcoming commentary on the narratives of Exodus (FOTL, 2).

10. For details on this exegesis, see my forthcoming commentary on the narratives of Numbers (FOTL, 4).

11. Coats, *Genesis*, 83.

12. Coats, *Genesis*, 170.

Notes to Chapter 6

A THREAT TO THE HOST

1. George W. Coats, *Genesis, with an Introduction to Narrative Literature* (FOTL, 1; Grand Rapids: Eerdmans, 1983), 109-13, 149-55, 188-92.

2. Martin Noth, *A History of Pentateuchal Traditions* (tr. Bernhard W. Anderson; Englewood Cliffs: Prentice-Hall, 1972), 263-64. See also Gerhard von Rad, *Genesis, a Commentary* (tr. John H. Marks; Philadelphia: Westminster, 1972), 167-70, 225-30, 271-73.

3. Noth, 105. See also Klaus Koch, *The Growth of the Biblical Tradition.* *The Form-Critical Method* (tr. S.M. Cupitt; New York: Charles Scribner's Sons, 1969), 111-32.

4. John van Seters, *Abraham in History and Tradition* (New Haven: Yale University Press, 1975), 173.

5. David L. Petersen, 'A Thrice-Told Tale: Genre, Theme, and Motif', *BR* 18 (1973), 30-43. Cf. also Koch, 116, 119.

6. Koch, 119. See also Klaus Koch, *Was ist Formgeschichte? Methoden der Bibelexegese* (3rd edn; Neukirchen-Vluyn: Neukirchener Verlag, 1974), 146.

7. See my commentary, 112, 151, 191.

8. Carl A. Keller, '"Die Gefährdung der Ahnfrau." Ein Beitrag zur gattungs- und motivsgeschichtlichen Erforschung alttestamentlicher Erzählungen', *ZAW* 66 (1954), 181-91. See also Petersen, 30; van Seters, 167.

9. Coats, 109, 149, 188. See also Koch, 111; Dixon Sutherland, 'The Organization of the Abraham Promise Narratives', *ZAW* 95 (1983), 341.

10. Von Rad, 169.

11. Claus Westermann, *The Promises to the Fathers. Studies on the Patriarchal Narratives* (tr. David E. Green; Philadelphia: Fortress, 1980), 122-24. Westermann sharpens the issue by observing, with Hoftijzer, that 'for each of the promise texts we must first inquire into its relationship to the narrative in which we find it or with which it is associated ... In the overwhelming majority of the passages in which we find a promise made to one of the patriarchs, this promise represents a secondary addition or interpolation.' The exegete cannot assume that since 'promise' is important for the context, it defines the intention of a particular pericope in that context. See also Westermann's treatment of the tales in *Genesis* (BKAT, 1; Neukirchen-Vluyn: Neukirchener Verlag, 1977); and Walter Brueggemann, *Genesis. Interpretation, a Bible Commentary for Teaching and Preaching* (Atlanta: John Knox, 1982), 126-29. Brueggemann places focal emphasis on the role of the promise for this tradition. But he also points to a different theme: 'The narrative makes clear that Abraham may indeed have the power to cause a blessing for an outsider. But Abraham also has the power to curse others.'

12. E.A. Speiser, *Genesis* (AB, 1; Garden City: Doubleday, 1964). See also his paper, 'The Wife-Sister Motif in the Patriarchal Narratives', in *Biblical and Other Studies* (ed. Alexander Altmann; Cambridge: Harvard University Press, 1963), 15-28.

13. Randy Chemberlin, *Selfishness: A Source of Strife in Genesis* (unpublished MDiv Thesis; Lexington Theological Seminary, 1984), 12-27.

14. Robert Polzin, '"The Ancestress of Israel in Danger" in Danger', *Semeia* 3 (1975), 81-97. Polzin builds his structural analysis on a dialectic established by interaction between images of adultery and wealth on the one hand and acquisition of progeny on the other. His pattern derives from the

larger context, the neighborhood for the story, which, he contends, the 'intellectuals' have failed to investigate. These opponents are people who pursue the diachronic relationships between the three versions of the story without considering synchronic relationships in the larger whole of the context. Yet, it seems to me to be a fundamental principle in method that one cannot draw conclusions about the larger context of a text without undergirding those conclusions with careful analyis of the text itself. Where in the story does the issue of progeny appear as an explicit element of the story?

15. The term refers to a nation of strength (Jer 50.41), a nation destined to grow from a patriarch, but with emphasis on special favor from God (Gen 46.3), indeed, to a nation that belongs to God (Deut 4.7, 8, 34). It implies people, not simply a patriarch. But the promise element has to do with the fame of the people, not with progeny. The promise to make the name great would be parallel (cf. Gen 11.4).

16. George W. Coats, 'The Curse in God's Blessing: Structure and Theology in the Yahwist', in *Die Botschaft und die Boten* (ed. Jörg Jeremias and Lothar Perlitt; Neukirchen-Vluyn: Neukirchener Verlag, 1981), 31-41.

17. Westermann, *Genesis*, 188. Westermann observes that the weight of the pericope rests on the speeches at the beginning and at the end of the unit. But the point is not a simple contrast between narrative description of an event and speech. To the contrary, speech can advance the description of event as well as narration of the event's process. The point is that neither narration nor speech focuses on an abstract argument, such as a defense of Abraham's claim that Sarah is his sister. Even in 20.12, where the speech carries Abraham's apology with an explicit explanation about Sarah's status as his sister, the explanation does not advance the story. Abraham's deception produces a threat to his relationship with his host, indeed, to the host himself. See Brueggemann, 129.

18. Van Seters, 168, emphasizes the entertainment dimension. Polzin, 83, ridicules the idea that the story could have been told for the delight of the tale. His objection focuses on the contention by 'form critics' that 'there must have been an intense pleasure experienced by the ancient Israelite when he was told how his father Abram "put a fast one over" on the lascivious Pharaoh who foolishly gives Abram much wealth and gets great plagues in return!'

19. Abraham is again guilty for his role in the plan. He called Sarah his sister in order to save his own neck (and to profit from the host's gifts). This element, like Gen 12, is not open strife, as in the Abraham–Lot stories. But it is a factor that causes strife and its corresponding separation. See the evaluation of this problem in Brueggemann, 129.

20. Polzin, 91.

21. Coats, *Genesis*, 129-32, 152-55.

22. Would this combination of motifs, famine forcing a trip to Egypt,

interrupted by theophany diverting the journey to Gerar, not be a combination of the two Abraham tales? See van Seters, 171-83. If the point can be defended, it would be difficult to see the Isaac story as the oldest element in the trilogy.
23. Noth, 105.
24. Noth, 105.
25. Van Seters, 183. Convincing objections about Noth's assumption concerning original units in a series defined by brevity must be heard. See Robert M. Polzin, 'Gerhard von Rad's *The Form-Critical Problem of the Hexateuch*', in *Biblical Structuralism. Method and Subjectivity in the Study of Ancient Texts* (Philadelphia: Fortress, 1977), 150-73. The objection does not vitiate the possibility, indeed, the necessity for finding the primary factor and thus the history of the tradition that defines relationships among texts in a single tradition.
26. One might refer here to Gen 22, a text that features the promise theme clearly as an after-thought. In vv. 15-18, the angel of the Lord calls to Abraham a second time, after the crisis of the story has been resolved, as if something had been forgotten in the resolution represented by the first round. And it is precisely in the second round that the promise theme appears. See my commentary, 157-62.
27. See the comments on this point above, and the information in note 16.

Notes to Chapter 7

NOVELLA

1. In fact, the novella and other longer narrative forms in the Old Testament have not received the attention accorded other genres by critical scholarship. No doubt this is in part due to the looseness of these forms and the variety within them.
2. A very useful discussion of these genre terms and their use in modern literary analysis is found in Hugh C. Holman, *A Handbook to Literature* (3rd edn; Indianapolis, New York: Odyssey Press, 1972), and has informed our discussion.
3. History, of course, can be well told and entertaining as well.
4. We are not concerned here with distinctions, great as they are, between historiography today and history writing in antiquity.
5. Herman Melville displays an exact knowledge of New England whaling practice in *Moby Dick*, but to read his masterpiece simply as a treatise on that subject would be to reveal a distinct failure of imagination. Just so, there may be a residue of historical material in the Joseph narrative, and reflections of relationships between tribes, but to deal with the narrative simply on these terms is to miss the primary thrust of the work. In fact,

William McKane (*Studies in the Patriarchal Narratives* [Edinburgh: Handsel Press, 1979], 72-74, 101-103) suggests that much that reflects tribal history (e.g. Gen 48) is secondary, breaking the flow of the narrative.

6. In this I differ from George W. Coats (*From Canaan to Egypt: Structural and Theological Context for the Joseph Story* [CBQ Monograph Series, 4; Washington: The Catholic Biblical Association of America, 1976]; 'Redactional Unity in Genesis 37–50', *JBL* 93 [1974], 15-21) who stresses the links between the Joseph narrative and its context and suggests that the 'transition is fundamental for the narrative of the story . . . the Joseph story was created from the beginning to serve this function . . . ' (*Canaan*, 77).

7. See W. Lee Humphreys, 'Joseph Story, The', *Interpreter's Dictionary of the Bible, Supplementary Volume* (Nashville: Abingdon Press, 1976), 491-92; George W. Coats, 'The Joseph Story and Ancient Wisdom: A Reappraisal', *CBQ* 35 (1973), 285-97.

8. Herman Gunkel, *The Legends of Genesis: The Biblical Saga* (New York: Schocken Books, 1967).

9. See Donald B. Redford, *A Study of the Biblical Story of Joseph (Genesis 37–50)* (VTSup, 20; Leiden: E.J. Brill, 1970), 87-100.

10. See Coats, *Canaan*, ch. 3.

Notes to Chapter 8

THE STORY OF ESTHER & MORDECAI

1. We here treat the Book of Esther as it appears in the Hebrew Bible and Protestant Old Testament. Later Additions to Esther were in time added to the book by some Jewish circles, and these are found in the Jewish and Protestant Apocrypha while appearing as part of the book in other Christian Old Testaments. These Additions alter the work in fundamental ways; on them see Carey A. Moore, *Daniel, Esther and Jeremiah: The Additions* (Anchor Bible, 44; Garden City, N.Y.: Doubleday, 1977).

2. For a different view see Sandra Beth Berg, *The Book of Esther* (SBL Dissertation Series, 44; Missoula: Scholars Press, 1979), 39-47.

3. *Table Talk*, xxiv.

4. See the general review in Carey A. Moore, *Esther* (Anchor Bible, 7B; Garden City, N.Y.: Doubleday, 1971), xxi-xxxi.

5. W. Lee Humphreys, 'A Life-Style for Diaspora: A Study of the Tales of Esther and Mordecai', *JBL* 92 (1973), 211-23. It is to correct this 'defect' that the Additions were in part made.

6. On this motif and its central role in the story see Berg, *Esther*, 31-37.

7. Theodor H. Gaster, 'Esther 1.22', *JBL* 69 (1950), 381.

8 See further Berg, *Esther*, passim; idem, 'After the Exile: God and History in the Books of Chronicles and Esther', in *The Divine Helmsman:*

Studies on God's Control of Human Events, Presented to Lou H. Silberman (ed. James L. Crenshaw and Samuel Sandmel; New York: KTAV, 1980), 114-20.

9. See Moore, *Esther*, xxxiv-xlvi, for a review of the evidence.
10. Compare the notices about Egyptian distaste for Hebrews and shepherds in Gen 43.32 and 46.34.
11. Moore, *Esther*, liii.
12. A 'defect' in some later eyes that was corrected by Additions stressing prayers by Esther and Mordecai in which they repent past sins, seek divine aid, recall past instances of God's deliverance, express confidence of divine control of events. Divine control is further noted in God's changing the king's rage to kindness and in a dream sent to Mordecai in which all is foretold, as Mordecai recognizes at the end.
13. See Berg, *Esther*, 173-84; 'After the Exile', 114-20.
14. See Humphreys, 'Life-Style,' 211-23; 'Esther, Book of', in *Interpreter's Dictionary of the Bible, Supplementary Volume* (Nashville: Abingdon, 1976), 280-81.
15. Berg, *Esther*, 169-73; Moore, *Esther*, lvii-lx.

Notes to Chapter 9

THE GENRE 'FABLE' IN THE OLD TESTAMENT

1. Robert Gordis, *Poets, Prophets, Sages: Essays in Biblical Interpretation* (Bloomington, Indiana: Indiana University Press, 1971), 34. That the term *māšāl* means political satire is quite apparent from Is 14.4, Mic 2.4 and Hab 2.6.
2. Stith Thompson, *The Folktale* (New York: Dryden, 1946), 10.
3. Lauri Honko, in 'Genre Analysis in Folkloristics and Comparative Religion', *Temenos* 3 (1968), 48-66, suggests nine criteria for defining a genre: content, form, style, structure, function, frequency, distribution, age and origin.
4. *Encyclopedia Britannica*, VII, 139 s.v. 'Fable'.
5. William Bascom, 'Folklore', *International Encyclopedia of the Social Sciences* (New York: Macmillan, 1968), V, 499. The lines between myth and folktale are easily crossed in a society where a divine reality appears in the form of an animal or a plant. Further definition must rely upon the social and cultural context of the story.
6. Therefore the story of the Garden of Eden in Gen 3 and Balaam's ass in Num 22 are excluded from the fable genre (*pace* J.L. Crenshaw, 'Wisdom Literature', in John Hayes [ed.], *Old Testament Form Criticism* [San Antonio: Trinity University Press, 1974], 246). The story of Jonah also is excluded on similar grounds.

7. Proverbs are primarily an Old World genre (Europe, Asia, Africa); see Bascom, 'Folklore'.

8. Alexander Krappe, *The Science of Folklore* (New York: Norton, 1964), 60-69.

9. On the other hand, Ruth Finnegan cautions against seeing 'moralizing tendencies' in African literature and prefers to call such morality common sense. Cf. here *Oral Literature in Africa* (Oxford: Clarendon Press, 1970), 378.

10. Krappe, 65.

11. For example, Krappe's remark about the lower popularity of plant tales (68) rests upon the assumption that both animal and plant fables are addressed to the same audience for the same moral purpose—an assumption I will disprove below.

12. In his work, *The Concept of Folklore* (Coral Gables, Fla.: The University Press of Florida, 1971), 98-108, Carvalho-Neto describes several of these changes in the process of what he terms 'aesthetic projection'. However, the nostalgic return to one's own past in a modern author's use of folklore, what he calls 'demophyletic [people-loving] simulation of folklore', is probably not the attitude or motivation of an author of sacred traditional literature, although the seventh century BCE may have been such a period of nostalgic return to origins in the ancient Near East. See also Archer Taylor, 'Folklore and the Student of Literature', in Alan Dundes (ed.), *The Study of Folklore* (Englewood Cliffs, N.J.: Prentice-Hall, 1965), 38.

13. Bascom, 'Folklore', 'Some Functions of Verbal Art', 498-500.

14. For example, Ivan A. Krylov's fables, first published in Russian in 1824 (*Basili*). A recent reissue of a translation is available: *Kriloff's Fables* (tr. T.C. Fillingham Coxwell; St Clair Shores, Mich.: Scholarly Press, 1970).

15. Cf. James Barr, *Comparative Philology and the Text of the Old Testament* (Oxford: OUP, 1978), and Phyllis A. Trible, *God and the Rhetoric of Sexuality* (Philadelphia: Fortress, 1978).

16. Perhaps the homophonous roots *māšāl*, 'to employ a fable', and *māšāl*, 'to rule over' are related to one another through the political fable itself. The question of who is to rule is certainly at the basis of the prophet's 'political oracles', which they refer to as *mᵉšālim*, e.g. Balaam's oracles (Num 23.9, 21; 24.7, 17, 20, 21, 23); Isa 14.4 and so on.

17. Finnegan, 323.

18. Finnegan, 363.

19. Bronislaw Malinowski, 'Myth in Primitive Psychology', in *Magic, Science and Religion and Other Essays* (Boston: Beacon, 1948), 72-124.

20. Bascom, 496.

21. *Encyclopedia Britannica*, VII, 132.

22. Finnegan, 346.

23. Georg Fohrer, *Introduction to the Old Testament* (Nashville: Abingdon, 1968), 314.

24. Finnegan, 376.

25. Von Rad; Crenshaw speaks of the form 'disintegrating into allegory', of it being 'completely dismantled'. This is an overstatement since the characters and mood are still the same.

26. The only culture which apparently does not have them is China (*Encyclopedia Britannica*, VII, 139), although the way in which nature is employed in the Chinese language and Taoist thought may provide a close analogy to the feelings, forms and functions of the fable. When *Aesop's Fables* were first published in China they were perceived as political satire, and were duly suppressed (Bascom, 500).

27. James Frazer, *Folk-Lore in the Old Testament* (London: Macmillan, 1919), II, 478.

28. Frazer, Hahn no. 125, 385, II, 478.

29. *Ancient Near Eastern Texts*, 592-93.

30. Bascom, 498ff.

31. Krappe, 68.

32. (Madison: University of Wisconsin Press, 1972).

33. Fraser, 306.

34. NEH Summer Seminar, Yale, 1981.

35. Fraser and Cole, 309.

36. Bascom, 284-85.

37. Juha Pentakainen, 'Religio-Anthropological Depth Research', in Richard M. Dorson and Alan Dundes (eds.), *Analytical Essays in Folklore* (The Hague: Mouton, 1975), 25-34.

38. J.A. Soggin, *Introduction to the Old Testament* (Philadelphia: Westminster, 1976), 52.

39. *Ibid.*

40. E.g. Artur Weiser, *The Old Testament: Its Formation and Development* (tr. Dorothea M. Barton; New York: Association Press, 1961), 63. Since Weiser does not recognize the political plant fable as a separate type, he must explain its political 'application' as a modification of its original meaning, and laments the loss of its 'independent significance'. Gunkel also failed to recognize the two types of fable, calling them all 'nature fables', examples of a primitive mentality far removed from our own (J.W. Rogerson, *Anthropology and the Old Testament* [Atlanta: John Knox, 1978], 80).

Notes to Chapter 10

JEHOASH'S FABLE OF THE THISTLE AND THE CEDAR

1. *A History of Israel in Old Testament Times*, (Philadelphia: Fortress Press, 1975), 214, 228, 233. Thus Herrmann is discounting the reference in 2 Kgs 15.1-2 and 2 Chr 26.3 to the fifty-two year reign of Amaziah's successor

Uzziah (Azariah), which would shorten Amaziah's reign to only a few years. For a slightly earlier dating of Jehoash and Amaziah, and a much shorter reign for Amaziah, see John Bright, *A History of Israel*, 467. Bright sees Jehoash's victories over Syria as part of a resurgence of power under the application of Assyrian pressure upon Damascus and Hamath, with Adadnirari crushing Damascus in 802 BCE, but not being able to follow up on the victory (pp. 237-38).

2. Herrmann, 238-40.

3. Contrast A. Alt's notion of 'charismatic monarchy', in 'The Monarchy in the Kingdoms of Israel and Judah', *Essays on OT History and Religion* (Oxford, 1966), 311-35.

4. E. Maly, 'The Jotham Fable—Anti-Monarchical?', *CBQ* 22 (1960), 299-305; H.H. Rowley, *The OT and Modern Study*, 93, and already J.G. Frazer, *Folk-Lore in the OT* (London: Macmillan, 1919), II, 472-73.

5. E.g. J. Bright and Montgomery, *The International Critical Commentary*, 440.

6. Any treatment of the broader literary unit in Kings must deal with the problem of resumptive repetition in 2 Kgs 13.12-13 and 14.15-16; the chiastic structure 2 Kgs 13.5, 13.25 and 14.27; the key words *panim*—'faces' and 'facing', 'counsel', and 'trample' and 'march'; and the message communication (see A. Vater, *The Communication of Messages and Oracles as a Narrative Medium* (Diss. Yale, 1976, exx. 102-104). The number of authors for Kings and Chronicles, their identities and their audiences' identities, are still under considerable discussion, but the foregoing reflections on 2 Kgs 14 and 2 Chr 25 may hopefully assist those tracking down the intervening stages between Jehoash and us (NEH Yale Seminar, 'Religion and Society in Ancient Israel', 1980).

INDEXES
INDEX OF BIBLICAL PASSAGES

INDEX OF AUTHORS

JOURNAL FOR THE STUDY OF THE OLD TESTAMENT
Supplement Series